WHAT THEY DIDN'T TEACH ME IN SUNDAY SCHOOL

WHAT THEY DIDN'T TEACH ME IN SUNDAY SCHOOL

ROB PARSONS

Hodder & Stoughton
LONDON SYDNEY AUCKLAND

Copyright © 1997, 2000 by Rob Parsons

First published in Great Britain in 1997
This edition first published in 2005

10 9 8 7 6 5 4

British Library Cataloguing in Publication Data
A record for this book is available from the British Library

ISBN 0 340 75618 7

Typeset by Avon Dataset Ltd, Bidford-on-Avon, Warks

Printed and bound in Great Britain by
Clays Ltd, St Ives plc

The paper and board used in this paperback are natural recyclable
products made from wood grown in sustainable forests.
The manufacturing processes conform to the environmental
regulations of the country of origin.

Hodder & Stoughton Ltd
A Division of Hodder Headline
338 Euston Road
London NW1 3BH

www.madaboutbooks.com
and www.hodderbibles.co.uk

To John Loosemore – who believed in me

CONTENTS

Before we start ...

Just before I wrote my first book somebody warned me that it was like giving birth – a strange mixture of pain and joy. They said the problem with publishers is that when you meet them, you want to know how your last baby is doing, but they want to know if you are pregnant! I have now given birth to five books, but, unlike in my real family, I have a favourite. Some of you may have read the *Sixty Minute* books on marriage and parenting. I loved writing those books and they are special to me. People from all walks of life, in multitudes of different situations, and with all shades of belief and non-belief, have written to say those books helped them; I am grateful for that. But it will not take you long to realise that this book is different. Here I share my deepest beliefs. Many of them have been carved out of times of pain and disappointment but each is precious to me.

I completely understand that your views may be

different from mine, or you may have no religious beliefs at all, but here are the things that matter to me. I have told my two children that in the years to come, long after I am gone, if they ever forget what mattered most to their father they can find it in this book. Here is my heart. This is my favourite child.

So many people have helped me give birth. Thanks to Jonathan Booth, Lyndon Bowring, Charlie Colchester, Sheron Rice, Tom Beardshaw, Lisa Curtis, Kate Hancock, Dr R.T. Kendall, Louise Kendall, Elizabeth McCusker, Peter Mortimer, and Steve Williams. As ever, special thanks and love to Dianne, Katie, Lloyd and Ron.

But above all, thank you to my Sunday School teachers; the older I get the more I appreciate what you gave me. I am sorry that I got into trouble so often in class. To avoid getting into even more, I have changed your names – with the exception of Miss Williams!

INTRODUCTION

THE BOY WHO WENT TO SUNDAY SCHOOL

I was four years old when Miss Williams called for me. My parents didn't go to church but had enlisted me in the Sunday School of the church on the corner of our street. During my time there many teachers would look after me, but Miss Williams, who supervised the infants' class, was the first.

Just recently that church celebrated its hundredth anniversary and the members invited me to say a few words at a Thanksgiving service. As I sat waiting to take part, my eyes gazed around the building. The old pews are long since gone and the large pulpit was taken down years ago, but so much was still the same and, as I allowed my mind to wander back down the years, the walls whispered their memories to me. Let me mention just two.

Sometimes our teacher would invite the class to tea

on a Sunday. My mother used to start preparing me for that occasion on the previous Monday. We didn't have a bathroom but the old tin bath would be dragged in from the garden, more times that week than in the previous month. As the moment drew closer she would try to put a small boy through the equivalent of a Swiss finishing school.

Finally the time would come – 4.15 on a Sunday afternoon. She would dampen my hair for the fifteenth time, thrust one of my father's handkerchiefs into my pocket and pass on a final word of exhortation. I can quite understand that at such a moment there are a million things a mother might want to say to her son; after all, he was leaving home for two hours to have tea with the Sunday School teacher. It often seemed that the responsibility of a last piece of advice would fluster her, and it would normally come down to, 'Remember, that if there's just one sandwich left – leave it.'

Oh those teas! Marmite sandwiches, jelly, blancmange and cup cakes. A grace that seemed to never stop and a television, on that day at least, that never started. But I loved those times. My teacher was saying to me, 'You are special. I care enough about you to invite you into my home – away from the varnished pews and the canvas-backed hymn books – into my private world.'

And then there was the Sunday School Outing. I can remember praying so hard the night before, that it would be fine. My young mind didn't consider that ten thousand farmers may have been praying for rain. In any event what did the national wheat harvest matter when you put it up against the Sunday School Outing?

It may be hard for a modern child to understand the wonder of that event. I confess, that as I look back, even I can't quite remember why the prospect of running around a muddy field, and dining on a bun and a glass of milk held such excitement.

But then as I sat in church on that anniversary day a strange thing happened. Suddenly I was back in Sunday School. I saw in my mind's eye not just Miss Williams but each of my old teachers in the clearest detail. Mr Clarke sat with a large black Bible on his lap and told me the story of David and Goliath; Mr Pendleton stared at me over the top of half-moon spectacles. He began, 'It was in the days of Pharaoh . . .' I would have worked my way through all ten teachers but just then a slide projector illuminated and the chairman began showing pictures of old Sunday school parties. And then suddenly there I was, aged seven. As I gazed at the child in the photograph I could not help but think, 'He had no idea what lay ahead; no notion of the pain and joys that were to come.' In truth, when I left Sunday School I had no idea that the learning process was only just beginning. There were things I couldn't learn at Sunday School.

Bill Cosby once said, 'You are more likely to remember your childhood than where you left your glasses.' He's right. I can still remember those lessons. But the reason they are so clear is that life itself has enforced them. I little knew, as Mr Clarke described a stone flying through the air, that one day as a man I would meet terrifying giants of my own. It was so for all my lessons.

★   ★   ★

When the anniversary service was over I walked down the aisle to make my way out. As I did so a silver-haired lady made her way to me and asked, 'Do you remember me?'

'Yes – of course!' I said. To my eye she seemed to have changed so little since she collected me on that Sunday afternoon all those years ago.

Miss Williams, and those faithful teachers who came after her, taught me well. I'm sure there were moments when they despaired that anything of real worth was being achieved in the heart of the inattentive boy who tried to make the others laugh. But God took what those faithful men and women taught the child and added what they could not teach me. In this short book I have highlighted some of them. There are, of course, other lessons, not mentioned here, but each of those that follow has been significant for me and, not a few of them, life-changing.

Like me, you may have memories of Sunday School, and if so you will surely remember some of your lessons. We should not be deceived by them. It may be that they were taught simply, but these were not simple lessons; they were profound. If we can only rediscover their power it will change the kind of homes we have, the businesses we run and even the governments we live under. In short, these lessons have the power to make the world a better place: your world.

As we begin our time together let me say something to two groups of people. First to a man or woman who has lost a faith that was once so real to them. You didn't intend to stop attending church but life became so busy, or perhaps somebody offended you one Sunday, or maybe you even experienced a life crisis that rocked your faith. As you read this little book, come back with me to your Sunday School days, back to being a child. Allow yourself a little time to consider how you lost what was so real to you all those years ago. The child you left behind can still teach you, still lead you, still stir again the flame of faith that has almost died in your heart. You can begin again. You can find afresh your first love.

And second, a word to every Sunday School teacher – especially those who may be finding it hard at the moment. Don't lose heart! Especially don't get discouraged as during the week you have the pressure of preparing those weekly lessons. Who knows how God will use that story? Remember, you are not moulding just a child, you are shaping a man, a woman. These kids will remember you *forever*.

I am now in my fifty-second year and yet with little effort I can imagine I am four years old again and Miss Williams is knocking on my door to take me to my first Sunday School. I hold her hand as we walk down the street together. Where is she leading this little boy, with new trousers, and slicked-down hair? She is leading him into the Bible – into the world of Peter who walked on water, and of the boy who brought his lunch to Jesus, and the world of the shepherd who became a giant killer. A new lesson every Sunday; a new Bible verse each week; a gold star for being good.

But Miss Williams and all those teachers who followed her did not only lead the child; they led the man. For the lessons they taught me all those years ago have borne fruit for almost half a century; I thank God with all my heart for every one of them.

CHAPTER ONE

THE KISS OF GOD

I once heard of a school teacher who at the beginning of every term used to send a letter home to the parents of the children in his class; it read, 'If you promise not to believe everything your child tells you goes on at school, then I promise not to believe all he tells me goes on at home.' It was a deal most parents were glad to sign in blood!

But, perhaps because we only saw them once a week, or, more likely, because they saw us only once a week, the relationship with our Sunday School teachers was so different to those we met at regular school. In truth most of them seemed like extra grandparents. To a child that hadn't hit double figures they certainly seemed old, but they were usually kind, and above all they had that quality that small children love: they didn't mind telling the same story over and over again.

And because they didn't mind telling it, and because we didn't mind listening, you could count on the fact that some week during a Sunday School term, we would sit enthralled and imagine that we were Joseph, the boy for whom the father made the special gift: the coat of many colours.

I was the youngest child in our family and so I knew what a privileged position Joseph was in. I have seen my older sisters sent to bed without supper because they wouldn't let me win at Monopoly. I don't feel proud of that now, but at the time it felt good; just about as good as to put on a coat that all your brothers wanted so badly they would kill for it.

Which of course is exactly what Joseph's brothers did; or at least thought they did. I can still see my Sunday School class sat in a circle as Mr Jenkins told us of the pit that the brothers threw Joseph in, and the eldest brother who pleaded for his life, and then the wandering gypsies who bought the young boy.

It wasn't hard to sympathise; there were bullies in my school who would have thrown you in a pit as soon as look at you, and even sold you to wandering travellers if they could have found any. But it was the sense of oneness with Joseph that made the last part of the story so delicious that we made Mr Jenkins tell it slowly: Joseph is second in command of the whole of Egypt, and his brothers come to him to plead for food; but they don't recognise him. It was as if every bully in our neighbourhood was lined up in front of us pleading for mercy except we were in disguise and they didn't know that we were the scrawny kid they beat up in the school-yard last Monday morning.

But then, just as Joseph has his bullying brothers where he wants them; just at the moment when he could crush them utterly, just as he has them at the place where he could wreak vengeance for all the sorrow they had been responsible for – the life in a strange country, the trumped-up rape charge, and the *years in prison – he forgives them. He doesn't even just forgive them; he makes it easier for them to forgive themselves and says, 'God meant it for good.'*

I remember discussing it on the way home from Sunday School. 'I wouldn't have given them anything to eat; I'd have dug the deepest pit in the whole world, and left them in it for fifty years, and then found the meanest wandering travellers and sold them all into slavery until they were dead.' Mr Jenkins' class wasn't too high on mercy in those days.

When I became a man I discovered that this wasn't a childish emotion but a human one. The desire to get revenge on your enemies is very old and very deep. But I remember with frightening clarity the day when men and women hurt me more than I thought possible and it dawned on me that the story I had heard from my Sunday School teacher's lips all those years ago wasn't just an ancient tale. I was really meant to do it. I was meant to do the unthinkable. I was meant to forgive them.

Gordon Wilson held his daughter Marie in his arms as she died. The place was Enniskillen in Northern Ireland; the bomb had gone off on Remembrance Sunday as hundreds of people stood to remember those who had laid down their lives in the service of their country. The next day a single word was being telephoned, faxed, copied around the news agencies of the world. That single word became the headline of newspapers across the United Kingdom; the man was interviewed on national television; such was its impact that the Queen referred to it in her Christmas broadcast that year; – the word was *forgiveness*. Gordon Wilson said that he forgave those who had killed his child. Not everybody agreed – there were not a few who said that to forgive like that was wrong – but whatever you believed, there was no doubt that we were witnessing something unusual, something almost from another world. Some said – almost Godlike.

Just recently I shared with a close friend a situation I felt I had handled badly. I had put it right as far as I could, but it still weighed heavily on me. When we finished talking I asked him to pray for me. I can't remember all of his prayer but one short phrase touched my heart. He said, 'Lord you have forgiven him. Help him to let go of it; *it's in the past*'.

'In the past' – just a common phrase and yet in those circumstances full of power. What my friend meant when he prayed with me that day is that ultimately what I did wrong I did against God and he has forgiven me. We sometimes hear people say, 'Oh, I have forgiven him but things can never be the same between us again.' But that is not how God forgives. Imagine you are a child again; you have hurt your father. He deals with you sternly and then, seeing your tears and knowing how sorry you are, he draws you to him. You cannot stop crying and you see his brow furrow as he searches for a way to tell you it is alright between you now. Then suddenly he leaves the room, but he is only gone a moment and when he returns he has in his hand a globe of the world. And then he kneels, looks you in the eye and says, 'Do you know how far the East is from the West? See, here is the

West . . .' Then his finger slowly moves around the circumference of the earth: you pass cities, countries, oceans, continents. Finally his finger stops, '. . . and here is the East. That is how far away I have put in my mind and heart what you did.[1] It is in the past; you and I must forget it now.'

One of the most powerful illustrations of that situation occurs in Dr Luke's record of the life of Christ.[2] Jesus is at a party held by a religious leader. In those days it was common courtesy to wash the feet of the guests, to give a kiss of welcome, and put a little oil on the head. Simon the Pharisee does none of these for the young teacher – it was a calculated insult. Somehow a woman, probably a prostitute, gets into the party. She is somebody whose life has been changed by Jesus and she begins to put right the insults to the man who had revolutionised her life. When the host sees this, he says to himself, 'This man is no prophet – if he was, he would know who she is and he wouldn't let her touch him.'

And it was at that moment that Jesus told his host a story. It concerned two men who owed sums to a money-lender. One owed a great deal of money and the other a much smaller amount. Neither could pay and the money-lender forgave them both the debts. When he had finished the story Jesus turned to his host, 'Now, Simon, which of them will love him more?'

The Pharisee was not a stupid man. 'I suppose the one who had the bigger debt cancelled.'

'You have judged correctly,' Jesus said.

When he looked back on what occurred next, Simon couldn't quite remember how it had happened. One moment he was answering an irritating question from the young carpenter, the next he was reeling as he realised this man was reading his very thoughts.

'Simon, do you see this woman? When I came into your house you did not give me any water for my feet, but she wet them with her tears and dried them with her hair. You did not kiss me, but she has not stopped kissing my feet. You did not put oil on my head but she has poured perfume on my feet. And Simon, she loves much, because she has been forgiven much. *But he who has been forgiven little loves little.*'

And then he turned to the woman and said words to her that nobody who heard them that day ever forgot. Simon remembered until he died the uproar they caused in his party; the guests remembered screaming at the carpenter, 'Only God can say those words!'

And every time the woman passed that familiar street corner, or saw a man's face that reminded her of the past, the words came back to her. He said, '*I forgive you.*'

I once saw a circus elephant tethered to a post with a thin piece of string. With a flick of its leg it could have easily torn the string and post from the ground but it didn't. And that is so because when the animal was young, the rope was attached to a chain which was wrapped around a post sunk deep into the ground. The young elephant tried hard to get free, but the rope never gave and it bit into him with every pull. And then one day the trainer removed the rope and chain and tied the elephant with string attached to a small stake in the ground. The elephant looked at it; it seemed so fragile.

But then old memories came flooding back. He believed that if he pulled the string, the pain would come. He decided he could not be free, and he would never try again.

Many of us live our lives tethered to the past, but Christ has died for us and we should be free. When we accept forgiveness through his death the ancient hold is broken. To live tied to the past is to live in a prison; it is to live carrying a weight on one's back; it is to sit like a bird in a cage gazing at blue skies through an *open* door.

In *Pilgrim's Progress* John Bunyan put it like this:

> He ran thus till he came at a place somewhat ascending, and upon that place stood a Cross, and a little below, in the bottom, a Sepulchre. So I saw in my dream, that just as Christian came up with the Cross, his burden loosed from off his shoulders, and fell from off his back; and began to tumble. And continued to do, till it came to the mouth of the Sepulchre, where it fell in, and I saw it no more.[3]

The parable of the prodigal son[4] has been called 'the greatest short story ever written'. It is captivating in so many ways but, for me, the heart of it, is the surprise. The boy gets to a stage where he knows he has made a dreadful mistake. The Jewish audience must have recoiled in horror as Jesus told how the son ended up in a pigsty. And he decides to make for home, but not as a son – he believes his days as a son are gone. He decides to ask for a job as a servant, and prepares a speech along those lines in preparation for the day he'll meet his father again.

What he doesn't know is that every evening since he left home, the old man has climbed onto the flat roof of the house and strained his eyes down the road to look for his boy. And when, one day, he sees him, he runs. The account has little sophistication in it – the old man is running and then falling on his son's neck and kissing him. The boy begins his speech, 'Father I am no more worthy to be called your son . . .' but he never finishes it.

The old man shouts, 'Put a ring on his finger, shoes on his feet and start the celebrations; my son is home again!'

You may know times like that in your walk with God. You will sit covered in shame in some pigsty somewhere and believe there is no way back. But he waits for you. You must be sorry for the past, you must want more than anything else to walk a different way in the future, but you must also remember you are his son, his daughter, and you should begin the long walk home.

Such forgiveness is hard to grasp. We live in a world where we are used to earning things – money, position, reputation. We have phrases like, 'Now you've proved yourself you can have more responsibility.' Much of that is not wrong, but the only thing you bring to the cross of Jesus is the wrong you have done; you cannot earn this forgiveness; this above all is free.

This is truly a great forgiveness but we can miss it. The great hope for the boy in the parable lay in the fact that he knew he was in a pigsty and far from the father's house. But it is possible to become self-righteous, to have lost a sensitivity to the Spirit of God, and therefore an understanding of our real condition. Somebody put it like this: 'Our churches are full of nice, kind, loving people who have never known the despair of guilt or the breathless wonder of forgiveness.'

As I was thinking about this concept some years ago, I had a picture of Jesus stalking down the corridor of a prison; on the doors were written the crimes that had been committed but he was flinging open prison doors and shouting, 'You can be forgiven!' And then the picture changed. The prison corridor was still there and he still stalked down it, but this time on the doors were written wrongs that policemen do not catch you for – greed and arrogance, pride and gossip, lack of love and a disregard of the weak; but to those, too, he shouted, 'You can be forgiven!'

But perhaps above all, we miss this forgiveness because we will not forgive those who wrong us. The words of Jesus could not be clearer, 'If you do not forgive those who hurt you, neither will your heavenly father forgive you.' At the heart of the Lord's prayer is the plea, 'Forgive us our sins, for we also forgive everyone who sins against us.'[5]

There was a man who owed a king a great deal of money and when he could not pay the king forgave him. That man then went out and found a man who owed him just a few pounds and, when he could not pay, had him thrown into prison. When the king heard of it he was angry and had the first man brought to him and said, 'I forgave you much, should you not also have forgiven?' And he turned him over to the jailers.[6]

To forgive others can be very hard. I remember realising very clearly that I had not forgiven somebody who had once hurt me badly. I had said I had forgiven him but I noticed that when others criticised him, I enjoyed it and caught myself saying, 'Me too – that's how he dealt with me as well.' I caught myself occasionally repeating to others the story of how he had hurt me, and discovered that rather than letting go of it I was, in fact, nursing it. It was *growing inside me.* That day I made a vow; it had several elements to it. First, I would never again raise the matter with anybody. Second, I would, whenever possible, try to speak well of this person. Third, I would not join in critical gossip about him. Fourth, I would, so far as he would allow, try to rebuild the relationship. Fifth, I would pray God's blessing on that man. As the years went by I felt my attitude to him soften and, perhaps, his did to me, for we were finally reconciled.

When we forgive it is not just for the sake of others. Often it is also *for our sake.* Dr R.T. Kendall of West-minster Chapel, describes an occasion in which he had been badly hurt.

It was at the time of my greatest trial and the result was my self-justifying feeling of resentment, bitter-ness and self-pity. I could talk to nobody about it except my wife. During this time an old friend, Josif Tson of Romania was passing through London and asked to see me. Little did I know this brief meeting was to be life-changing.

Since he was from outside London (and nobody would know) I told him what they did to me. I poured my heart out and told him all I could think of. 'Is there anything more?' he asked. 'No, that's it,' I said.

Josif asked for fifteen minutes to take a brief nap and hoped I'd have a cup of tea ready for him. When he returned he took a sip of tea, then he pointed a finger at me. 'RT,' he began firmly in his lovely Romanian accent, 'You must totally forgive them. Until you totally forgive them, *you will be in chains*. Release them and you will be released.'

I said, 'Josif, I just remembered something else they did that I haven't told you.' But he was not interested in more of my self-pity. 'RT, you must totally forgive them. Release them and you will be released.'

It was my biggest test – the hardest thing I have ever had to do. But Josif was right – I was in chains and when I released them, I was free.

Sometimes this releasing of others is a gradual process. We wish that we could do it immediately but sometimes it is a build-up of small victories. We believe we have let them go but then suddenly the memory of the hurt comes flooding back and we feel the old bitterness rising in our hearts. It is then we need to release them afresh, and begin again. Such forgiveness is always hard, for sometimes, as you cry 'forgive them' they are still banging nails into your hands and feet.[7] But it is our only hope of freedom, of being loosed of the chains of bitterness. The Chinese have a proverb: 'The one who will not forgive must dig *two* graves.'

There may be occasions when we have to forgive

those who don't even know they have wronged us. We felt the hurt deeply but if we went to them and said, 'I forgive you for what you did' they wouldn't know what we were talking about. In these cases it is often best to say nothing; simply release them.

Sometimes it is hard to forgive because those who have wronged us show no regret; it seems at times that, given the chance, they would do it all again. In these circumstances it is very important to understand what forgiveness is not. It is not saying to them, 'What you did doesn't matter.' When Gordon Wilson in Enniskillen said he forgave those who had killed his daughter, he was not releasing them from the fact they will have to answer to God. He did not have the authority to do that.

We live in a moral universe in which men and women, unless they themselves have sought his forgiveness, will one day account for their actions before God. One of the most poignant newspaper cartoons of World War II was set in a concentration camp. A line of Jewish people were being mown down by a stormtrooper with a machine-gun. Behind the soldier was a colonel who had a notebook and pencil and who was making a list of names and dates as the victims fell. But the soldier's face was half turned to a figure in white who stood behind the colonel. The colonel could not see him, but in the angel's hand was a notebook and a pencil, and he was recording . . . names and dates.

We know almost nothing about the man we meet in the Gospels on the day that Jesus died. We are told he was a thief, and it was for that reason he was pinned with nails to a cross next to the young carpenter. We know that, whatever wrong he had done in his life, with his dying breath he sprang to the defence of the man the whole world seemed to want to kill. And we know that he yelled out, 'Jesus, remember me!'[8]

And it was then that Jesus said something to him that has brought freedom and hope to millions of people down the generations and will go on doing so. He said, 'Today you will be with me in paradise.'[9]

Wonderful words! – 'Today', 'with me', 'in paradise' – a Persian phrase that meant 'the garden of God'. But better than all of that, was the implication that said to him, 'Everything that holds you to that cross I forgive. You are pinned with nails but – for the first time in your life – you are free.'

> On the Mount of Crucifixion
> Fountains opened deep and wide;
> Through the floodgates of God's mercy
> Flowed a vast and gracious tide.
> Grace and love, like mighty rivers,
> Poured incessant from above,
> And heaven's peace and perfect justice
> Kissed a guilty world in love.[10]

There is no message in the world like this: it can set you free and, if you live in the good of it, keep you free.

It is the kiss of God.

CHAPTER TWO

I AM KNOWN COMPLETELY AND LOVED UNCONDITIONALLY

Sunday School ended at 3.30 p.m. and our evening 'gospel meeting' started at 6.30 p.m. Sometimes in the evenings there would be a baptism and if ever that was the case then Sunday School would get interrupted by the preparations. Our baptistry was sunk into the floor and covered with boards and carpet. Whenever it was needed the Sunday School superintendent would move the classes that met at that end of the church so the deacons could get the tank filled with water, and put in the portable water-heater that was designed to ensure we didn't lose any new believers to hypothermia.

When all was prepared they always left the baptistry filled and . . . open. And that in itself would not have been a problem but for the fact that Mrs Manley walked in carrying a tray of biscuits. Due to my age I wasn't there the first time that Mrs Manley got baptised, but I am sure that she could not have had a more attentive audience than she did on the second occasion.

Our joy at being able to witness the sight was only slightly tempered by the vision of all those delicious biscuits floating on the water.

That memory and a hundred others are seared into my mind. They come back to me with greater clarity than what I did last week (a lot greater clarity). I remember silver stars for bringing a Bible and gold stars for getting the questions right. I worked for three years to get enough stars for the major prize; when I was eleven I realised you could buy stars at the newsagents.

And I remember Mrs Price's promise box. It was a small cardboard container that held hundreds of tiny pieces of rolled paper; on each piece was a Bible promise. Just next to it on the large brown table were a pair of tweezers and we were occasionally allowed to go hunting for a promise. Looking back now, it doesn't seem the most exegetical way of getting one's theology, but it certainly had an element of excitement. And one day I got a promise that has sustained me through some of the darkest years of my life. 'I will never leave you nor forsake you.'

Mrs Price drove it home: 'Rob, that means never. You are his and he is yours. Nothing can ever separate you from his love. There is somebody who knows you better than you know yourself and loves you. You have a friend for life.'

I thank God for those people: for the way they occasionally fell into baptistries, and the way they could make a nine-year-old boy carry a big black Bible down his street just to get a silver star. And I thank God that Mrs Price had a promise box.

I heard of a man who as a boy never felt affirmed by his

father. His father's critical spirit made him wonder if he had ever been accepted as a son. He was in his mid-forties and married with children of his own, when one day his father, whom he had not seen for five years, telephoned to say he was about to visit. He panicked; he now had a beard and he knew his father would not approve. The old man was due to arrive in five days' time and on each of those days the son argued with himself over whether or not he should shave off his beard. He found himself talking to himself, 'You're a father yourself now. You must make your own decisions.' But at ten o'clock in the morning on the day his father was due to arrive, he shaved off his beard.

He waited on a crowded train station and suddenly saw his father walking towards him. He smiled and went to shake his father's hand but hesitated as he saw the old man's brow furrow. His father said, 'Nice to see you son. But aren't those sideboards a little long?'

At that very moment he knew that nothing had changed. This was still the man he could not please. Many of us have lived our Christian lives as though God is a father like that. The day we discover differently is the day we begin to live. This could be your day.

I have spoken to thousands of people during the coffee breaks in our seminars but for some reason my conversation with one man remains as clear as if it were yesterday. He was about forty years old. He said, 'I'm a director of a company, I have two hundred people working for me, I have three children of my own. By most standards people look at me and say that I'm successful'. And then he dropped his voice and whispered, 'Tell me why I am still trying to prove myself to my father.' He told me that when he was a teenager he had come running in from school anxious to tell his father that he had come second in a music examination that included candidates from the whole of his county. His father had listened to his son's enthusiasm and then asked, 'Won't you ever come first?'

Many Christians live like that man. They believe that God is their father, they believe they came into that relationship because of faith. If you asked them whether it is possible to earn God's love they would tell you they are trusting in the grace of God. But in reality they spend their lives trying to earn that love. God becomes for them the father they can never please, the one who always has another demand up his sleeve, the one they are forever disappointing.

These people have forgotten the number of times they have rededicated their lives to God, and their book-shelves bear evidence to the efforts of the years to find the magic formula which will turn them into the kind of Christian that God will be proud of. There have been times when they have risen from bed before it was light and prayed until their knees hurt, and moments when they have almost read the Bible in a year, but even then he seemed to want more.

One man wrote to me and put it like this:

I attend church as well as another class every Sunday. I read the Bible and pray wherever I am, I go to prayer and praise at our minister's house every Wednesday and to another meeting on a Monday evening. Do I sound like a good Christian? This question has really puzzled me so I hope you

> will be able to help me. I am trying hard to be a
> good Christian and I'm more than ever involved in
> the church. Do you think I am doing enough?
> Thank you for taking the time to listen to me.[1]

I have tried to imagine this man striving hard to please
God but all the time there is the nagging doubt that he
will never be good enough. I have no doubt he listens to
good preachers, reads helpful books, and determines to
progress in his faith but there is rarely a sense of God's
approval. If nobody helps him he will die wondering if
he ever really made it.

I once saw a school photograph that saddened me
deeply. It was of a large group of children at the beginning of their teen years. The girls were already looking
like women in the making, the boys like . . . large boys.
But one girl caught my attention. She was very over-
weight and sat with her hands on her knees. She did
not have a pretty face, but she smiled out from behind
thick spectacles. I asked my friend's child to tell me
about her. Apparently, she had few friends because,
among other things, she smelt a little and some of the
children would not sit by her. She was not good at
sport and regularly came somewhere near the bottom
of the class in terms of academic achievement. Whenever the teacher asked two leaders to pick teams, she
was always the last one chosen and invariably one
captain would say, 'You can have her.'

And as I looked at her, I felt a great emotion well up
in me. I wanted to hold her, to tell her that she was
somebody. I wanted to find something in that child's life

that she could do moderately well and praise her for it. I wanted to tell her I would always be her friend, and I would love to sit next to her.

Not long ago I received a poem. It is called 'Picking Teams'.

> When we pick teams in the playground
> Whatever the game might be
> There's always somebody left till last
> And usually it's me.
>
> I stand there looking hopeful
> And tapping myself on the chest
> But the captains pick the others first
> Starting of course with the best.
>
> Maybe if teams were sometimes picked
> Starting with the worst
> Once in his life a boy like me
> Could end up being first.[2]

Another child put it like this: 'Heaven is a place where there are no teams and nobody ever gets picked last.'

But many of us have never left the playground; we still secretly believe that God will only love us when we do well. The mind-blowing concept of grace – God's unmerited favour towards us – is hard for us to grasp in a society used to earning love. The truth is that the message of the gospel is a surprise; it runs counter to much we have been taught and almost all that we have experienced in other relationships. *God knows you and*

God loves you. He loved you when you were his enemy and he loves you now you are his child.

Many of us find it hard to live in the good of this and so struggle all our lives trying to earn the very love of God. But when we live that way we are destined to live a weary Christian life, for proving yourself to God is the most draining lifestyle of all. When we reach extremes of this position it is hard to even believe that God is on our side. Only those who have woken each day with the daunting prospect of earning God's love have known the trauma of trying to achieve it.

I was a Christian for many years before I realised this. I used to live my Christian life as though God was constantly looking over the balcony of heaven just waiting for me to prove myself to him.

Some days I would feel as though I had done pretty well. I'd prayed, been gracious to the miserable man in the office next to me, and made the evening meeting at church. But as I fell into bed at the end of such a day did I feel liberated? No, it had been a long hard slog and I knew in my heart that I probably wouldn't be as 'spiritual' the next day.

And then one day somebody gave me some news that changed my life. He said the simple words, 'God is *for* you! He's for you when you succeed and when you fail. He's for you when your heart is filled with certainty and your head is filled with doubt. He's for you when you share the faith with thousands and when you deny him. God is for you – *he is on your side!*'

Now there's a revolutionary thought – *God is on our side.* The Bible tells us that nothing will ever separate us from the love of God – demons can't and angels won't.[3] Does he want us to spend time in prayer, to get to church meetings and to share our faith with others? Yes, but if we do them all he could not love us more, and if we miss them all he will not love us less.

This concept is so alien to our culture it is almost a daily battle to keep hold of it. But once we grasp it we find weights we have carried for many years begin to fall away. Somebody described it like this, 'Suddenly I felt an incredible freedom. It had dawned on me I did not have to prove myself to God. I felt not only loved, but a fresh love for him rising in me. How could I not love someone who had loved me unconditionally?'

I was at the door of the auditorium, shaking hands with people as they left when she came up to me. I had been talking about the power of unconditional love and it was obvious that something I had said had touched this woman's heart but I am in her debt, for the story she told me that day has never left me.

She was a single parent and her son was twenty-three years old. She had tried hard to encourage him in the Christian faith and he used to go to church but somebody had offended him and he had stopped attending. She told me her son was a punk rocker. In fact he was the most outrageous punk rocker in the whole of her city. His head was shaved apart from a piece in the centre which stood up like the tail of a cockatoo and was bright orange. He wore a ring through his nose and cheek. He dressed in leather and wore a little mascara.

The previous week he had been helping her shop in

a local supermarket and they were at the check-out when he said, 'I'm going to get some cigarettes. Then I'll come back and help you pack.'

The moment he left, the woman at the check-out said, 'How can you bear to be seen out with him when he looks like that?'

The single-parent mum said to me, 'I smiled at her and said, "Oh, my dear, it's very easy. You see I have brought him up through all these years. I love him. *He's my son.*" '

We can be moved by a story like this but it is still hard to believe that the God who knows us intimately – better than we know ourselves – should love us in such a way.

Some years ago a friend called at my home; he knew that I was going through a very difficult time. It was a Sunday morning and he asked if I minded missing church. I said, 'Not at all.' We talked together about handling criticism and how it was possible to feel of no value. And it was then that he said something that has remained with me until today. He told me there were lots of rumours spreading across the country about him. They were untrue, tiresome and hurtful. One night he had cried out to God, 'Lord these rumours are hurtful!' And it was then he felt God say to him: 'They're not as bad as the truth; *and I know the truth and I still love you.*'

One night I gave a closing address at a Christian conference. I had preached on the fact that God knows the worst about us and yet loves us unconditionally – that he is our father. When I had finished I took my seat alongside the two men who were chairing the event.

And then one of them made his way towards the microphone and told a most powerful story. Here is the event Jeff Lucas spoke of that night as told in his book, *Walking Backwards*:

I picked up the phone and my fears were confirmed: Dad was dying. I was to cancel everything and rush home immediately on the next plane . . . Two hours later, I rushed into Dad's hospital room. He was conscious and, as I took his hand and smoothed his hair, he smiled but said nothing. My dad had been unable to speak for some four years. He loved to talk but that gift had been taken from him by a stroke which reduced his speech to meaningless drivel.

Now, as I sat at his bedside, I knew that time was short. 'Dad, I love you so very much. You know that don't you?' He smiled, but then his eyes clouded over. I could see he was struggling to say something important but the words wouldn't come out. However, he had overcome this handicap before. My dad knew how to communicate without words.

Some months earlier I'd been staying overnight at my parents' home. It was the end of the day and I had already retired to my room. There was a knock on the door. Dad came in and knelt down silently by the bed. He took the blankets and the sheets and tucked me in, just like he'd done thirty-five years earlier when I was his five-year-old. With a kiss on my cheek, brushing away a stray hair on my face, he was gone. I lay there in the dark, aware that here was I, a forty-year-old adult, so used to making decisions and fending for myself and my family, and I had just been tucked in and made warm and secure by my frail father. It felt good.[4]

Jeff then looked out at four thousand people and said, 'God wants to tuck some of you in tonight – to let you know again that you are loved.' As he spoke I watched the audience. I could both see and feel emotion bursting out all over the arena. Grown men and women were realising, some for the first time in their lives, that God loves them.

I have many close friends, some of whom I believe may even die for me. But they do not know me. They know parts of me and some of them may know me better than I know myself. But there is one who both knows me completely and yet loves me utterly. I am sometimes a disappointment to him, but never a surprise. It is that knowledge which leads us into the next lesson: there really is nothing to prove.

God is *for* you.

Chapter Three

The greatest freedom is in having nothing to prove

Sometimes I close my eyes and imagine I am back in Sunday School. Even now, after all these years, I can transport myself back to that little church on the street corner and the room at the top of the building which housed my class. In my mind's eye it is a hot summer afternoon and the sun is streaming in through the tall windows, catching specks of dust in its beams and making them dance. I fancy I can still hear the old pedal organ that the teacher pounded furiously; it always seemed either tired or just plain cross at being woken. I remember hymn-books that were covered in what looked like linoleum; and I can't just remember those books – I can smell them.

I have often tried to understand what it was that so drew me to Sunday School. Television had been invented (one of my kids asked me recently whether radio had been invented!) and there were a hundred and one other things that at least on the surface looked a whole lot more fun. But I never missed.

I think the answer is probably very simple and actually just as relevant today: my Sunday School teacher made me feel special. She made me feel I had the capacity to ruin her whole day by playing truant.

Whenever I came into the class she would ask me about my week. I smile now as I think of this dear lady's sudden interest in football. And whenever I answered one of her questions about the Bible she never made me feel silly if I got it wrong; she had the ability to make every child's reply seem worthwhile. Sometimes that was easier than others, such as when Peter Harries said that the seventh commandment was, 'Humour thy father and thy mother.'

So there it is – our Sunday School teacher accepted us; with her there was nothing to prove. She accepted David who was clever, and Simon who was slow. She never treated Karl, whose father was a managing director, differently from Tom whose dad was a bus driver. I remember thinking, I'll bet God is like my Sunday School teacher.

It all began in the nursery. Claire was just six months old when the toothless face leant over the cot and said, 'Smile for grandad.' Claire did not feel like smiling; she'd had an awful night. Every time she whimpered her parents had leapt into her bedroom, yanked her out of the cot and started to bounce her up and down. And this morning had begun badly. The usual milk was apparently off the menu and instead they had served up something that, if she hadn't been sure her parents loved her, she could have sworn was stewed prune. Claire was not happy.

Nevertheless the toothless old gentleman still called down to her, 'Smile for me!' She was just about to throw a heavy rattle at the old man when she felt the wind in her stomach and her face involuntarily broke into a huge grin. And it was then that something happened which was to affect the whole of Claire's life. Her grandfather yelled, 'She's done it! She smiled for me.' As a reward he passed down a cuddly toy and then rushed off to get other adults to witness the phenomenon. Soon there was only standing room around the cot as various members of the family stared down, hoping for a repeat of the wonder.

Claire gazed up, thought, *Why not?* – and broke into a wide smile. The crowd went wild – they clapped, patted her on the head, and, most important of all, inundated the cot with goodies.

At the tender age of six months, eleven days, and fourteen hours, Claire Emma Taylor had learnt a lesson that was to mould her whole life: *You can make people like you by what you do; it really is possible to earn love.*

Most of us never manage to completely unlearn that lesson and when we are finally laid to rest it is at the end of a life that has been dominated by the desire, and even the need, to prove ourselves to somebody. By that time the sheer effort involved in that pursuit has left us physically and emotionally exhausted; before we slip away we have only strength for one last thought – *I wonder how many people will come to my funeral?*

Whilst a feeling of unworthiness will rob some of us

of peace, the desire to earn love drives many of us into lives of furious activity. We come to believe that the only way to be loved – accepted, even – is to perform well. The strange thing is that success does not fulfil that need, it rather fuels it as we are driven to prove ourselves in even greater tasks. Failure, or even a little criticism, can crush us utterly.

I have learned that being a Christian does not necessarily exempt us from this kind of lifestyle. I have lived it for much of my life; even now, although its hold seems weaker, it is an ongoing battle. And battle it is, for this way of living can kill not only your body, but has the ability to slowly strangle your inner spiritual life. This is how one man put it:

> Work had always been highly esteemed in our family, and hard work was seen as the primary tool for success. I figured if it was good to work ten hours, it would be even better to work fourteen . . .
>
> I would come home feeling that I hadn't worked enough. So I tried to cram even more into my schedule . . . My life wasn't abundant, it was a frantic sprint from one hour to the next.
>
> I can remember times when fatigue left me feeling isolated and alienated – feelings that previously had been foreigners to me . . . I became frustrated and laughter, which had always been my most treasured companion, had silently slipped away.
>
> I was dominated by 'shoulds' and 'ought tos' and 'musts'. I would awaken unrefreshed in the morning, with a tired kind of resentment, and

hurry through the day trying to uncover and meet the demands of others. Days were not lived but endured. I was exhausted trying to be a hope constantly rekindled for others, straining to live up to their images of me. I had worked hard to build up a reputation as one who was concerned, available, and involved – now I was being tyrannised by it. Often I was more at peace in the eyes of others than in my own.

Hurry needs answers; answers need categories; categories need labelling and dissecting. The pace I was trying to maintain had no time for rhythm and awe, for mystery and wonder . . . In order to keep up my incessant activity, God was simply reduced to fit into my schedule. I suffered because he didn't fit.[1]

Such a person is often popular and that very popularity can so often mask the great tragedy going on in the heart. We have managed to build a reputation as a man or woman who gets things done. We are in demand to sit on committees, to organise functions, to teach Sunday School, to do anything and everything. We have long since given up going to church to worship. No, we go now to push agendas forward; there are people to see, things to organise. As the preacher speaks we are jotting down the names of the people we need to see when the service is over but we need not have worried for, even as we open our eyes after the final prayer, there is a long line of people wanting a minute of our time. We are needed. The word that is always on our lips is, 'yes'.

'Yes, of course I can sit on that committee.'

'Yes, I'd be pleased to help in any way I can.'

'You only have to ask – you know I'd love to help.'

In truth we are back in the nursery yelling to anyone who will listen, 'I'm smiling – come and see me smile. I am trying hard to make you love me.'

The great tragedy of this situation is that so often whilst we are saying 'yes' to the whole world, we are saying 'no' to those who need us most. I have made so many mistakes in this area. I remember being so busy when the children were small that I just didn't have time for my own family. Was I popular? You'd better believe it! At times I could almost hear people saying, 'Oh, he's such a gifted speaker. He's so willing to help. He's always there when we need him.' And that may have been fine had the great speaker spent a little more time communicating with his own family. It may have been acceptable if the one who was so willing to help others had heard his own wife's cries for help a little earlier, and if the man who was 'always there when we need him' had been more available to those for whom he had primary responsibility.

Some years ago I received an anonymous letter from a church leader's wife. It contained a poem. She has never known how often I have read it and cried in my heart for her. It moved me because I have no doubt this woman loves her husband but he has no idea what his busy life is doing to their relationship. She is reaching out from her very soul:

I want my husband to smile again.

I want to be able to talk to him after dinner.
I want for our family to go out on Saturdays for a walk
    or a shopping trip.
I want to be me – not 'the minister's wife'.
I want to sit in church, listen to the notices, and
    decide what *I would like to go to.*
I want my husband to come home at night and relax
    instead of just recharging the batteries and disap-
    pearing out again.
I want to celebrate birthdays, and anniversaries
    always, not just when there are no church meetings.
I want to be able to tell the self-centred and self-
    righteous folk that they are.
I want him to come in at night and talk to us instead
    of slumping silently reliving the awkward visit or
    difficult meeting he's been at.
I want people to stop telling me how wonderful it
    must be to be the minister's wife and then
    complain they've not had a visit for months.
I want people who regularly miss meetings because
    they've 'had a busy day' to let us miss occasional
    meetings because we've 'had a busy day'.
I want him to come with me sometimes to see our
    child swim or play football.
I want him to be my husband instead of their minister.
And I want not to be guilty about these things.[2]

At the bottom of the poem is a PS, 'Tonight is one of
those nights when it is all too much for me. I hope that
you will read this and maybe pray for us even though
you don't know us.'

Who is this woman who has written to a stranger
with such a cry from the heart? Where does she live,

and is life better for her and their child now? Is her husband still so busy, and is this busyness producing fruit or barrenness?

A lifestyle of busyness and over-commitment has one particular characteristic: whatever we do, it will never be enough. I once received a letter from a woman who described what she called 'the agony' of trying to be the 'perfect mother' in the eyes of her in-laws.

And what if we do manage to please people? One would have thought that those of us who live this way would be thrilled when we achieve a goal. And we are – for a very *little* while. Somebody compliments us on a job we have done and we feel a fleeting glow of pleasure, but almost immediately an inner voice whispers, 'Will I do the next job as well?' We may be a church leader and smile as the member of the congregation says, 'I enjoyed your sermon today; God spoke to me.' But as she moves away and we extend our hand to greet the next person, an inner voice asks, 'Will I be as compelling next week?' In truth, whether we are church leaders, students, sales executives or homemakers we are constantly asking ourselves, 'Can I go on pleasing you – will you approve of me tomorrow?'

The constant need to prove ourselves, to earn acceptance and even love is utterly draining. Those of us caught on its treadmill have no resting place for we must always be on to the next thing. We know little satisfaction at what we have achieved. We have no inner peace. We even feel guilty when we try to relax. Holidays are often not an oasis but something to be endured until we can get back to the security of activity.

I remember one church leader confiding to me that he worried if he went to the park with his wife and children in an afternoon in case a member of his congregation saw him and thought he was shirking. The fact that he works evenings, all day Sunday and rarely takes holidays didn't figure in his thinking. He is in the prison of , 'What will they think?' and, although it is sad, I understand it completely – I've spent a sentence or two there myself.

The symptoms of the driven life – distorted sense of worth, restlessness of spirit, inability to enjoy success or even to relax – are miserable enough. But there is a greater, more terrifying, factor in the driven life; such a person has the ability to run on empty for years. Long after the reality of faith has died in the heart and years after any real sense of communion with God has gone, the driven life prays, sings, organises, preaches, gives financially – in fact does anything that involves 'doing' rather than 'being'. The great tragedy is that whilst others are fooled he or she is usually not so deluded. They know what has happened; they have died inside.

THEIR FIRST DAY IN HEAVEN

The three of them were at the gates,
all togged up in their new wings.
'I wonder if we'll sing?' said Herbert.
Mrs Gee and Herbert looked at their heavenly mate
  and Herbert said in his Sunday voice,
'My name is Herbert Hodgkinson – deacon at the
  South Sea Mission,

Chairman of the Billy Graham inter-college Christian
    Union,
Sunday School inspector for the whole of Yorkshire
    East,
Co-ordinator of the Federation of British Whitsun Treats,
Teacher, preacher, evangeliser, prophet, priest
    and . . .'

'My name's Bartholomew. On earth I knew . . .'
'Pleased to meet you!' came the rushing wind of Mrs
    Gee,
organiser of the local 'Save the Natives' tea,
Women's Guild and sewing class,
Christian croquet on the grass.
Healthy, red and rosy, she.

'My name's Bartholomew,' said he,
'On earth I knew . . .'

'You ever preached at Bognor Hall?'

'I never preached nowhere at all.'

'Does your wife arrange flowers for the local church?'

'No . . . left me and three kids years ago – left us in
    the lurch.'

And Mrs Gee turned to dear Herb and said,
'Why, this is strange and so absurd.
This little man with scars, and wounds and dirty face.
I must say, Herb, he's out of place.
And blood all over his new wings.
It shows a life of awful sins . . .'

But then *he* came.
A light so bright that all three cringed before the King
of Heaven.

It was Herbert who recovered first and soon began
his usual burst:
'I'm Herbert Hodgkinson, chairman . . .'
'And I'm Mrs Gee, *surely* you remember me.'

But then he spoke, 'Bartholomew, it's good to see
you. Come with me.'

And Mrs Gee quite red with rage turned on St Peter
to complain,
'Why him? Why him? It's so absurd . . .'

'Shhh . . . they knew each other . . . back on earth.'

Can we change? Yes, but it is not an easy road. We do
not easily give up the security of the life that earns its
approval, and even its love, by doing. Sometimes what
causes us to change is the welfare of those around us. It
may be a close family member, perhaps our husband
or wife, begins to crack under the strain. The strange
thing is that those of us living a frantic lifestyle often
cope reasonably well for a while; it is those around us
who pick up the real cost. I have seen many people
begin the search for a different way to live when they
have seen what the present style is doing to those they
love.

And some change because of illness. The headaches,
the stomach pain, the irritability and the hostility that

so often accompany this way of life gradually increase, and finally our body says 'enough'. And now we have to be quiet, perhaps even confined to bed, and this gives us time to do the one thing that most of us manage to avoid for a lifetime – we begin to think.

Some time ago, at a seminar I was running I met a lawyer. He told me that a car crash in which he had almost lost his life and which left him hospitalised for six months, changed him completely. He said, 'I used to carry photographs of my children around to remind myself what they looked like. But the office survived without me, and I began to see the things that really mattered to me.' This is how one church leader described such an experience:

> On Tuesday I picked up my diary to review the week's schedule: four seriously ill people to call on, my own doctor's appointment, several requests for counselling, a sermon outline for the church bulletin to be completed by tomorrow morning, a fund-raising letter to be written to the congregation by Thursday, five meetings scheduled between Tuesday evening and Friday noon. On Friday night and Saturday I was speaking three times to our leadership training class, on Sunday preaching twice. My Sunday sermon was, 'Doing what you can' but I knew I was way beyond that. I survived the week by postponing some visiting, giving up my day off and cancelling two meetings. My wife said, 'You have made this church your mistress.' But what could I give up? How could I change?

He then became seriously ill and thought that he might lose his life. He spoke of that experience:

> I have never had so much time to think, and the words that came repeatedly to my mind were limits and finitude. The conflict between my racing mind and wild emotions and helpless body forced me to realise that if I were going to live and recover my ministry my priorities required a major overhaul. What did God want to teach me about a different style of life and ministry?[3]

Some years ago I was battling over these same issues: I wanted peace yet desperately needed the affirmation I thought I'd find through sheer activity. Then a friend showed me something he had just read. I didn't know the author but he had written about me:

> When I took a closer look at this I realised that I was caught in a strange web of paradoxes.
> While complaining about too many demands I felt uneasy when none were made.
> While speaking about the burden of letter writing, an empty mailbox made me sad.
> While fretting about giving lecture tours, I felt disappointed when there were no invitations.
> While speaking nostalgically about an empty desk, I feared the day when that would come true.
> In short, whilst desiring to be alone, I was frightened of being left alone.
> The more I became aware of these paradoxes the more I started to see how much I had indeed fallen in love with my own compulsions and

illusions, and how much I needed to step back and wonder, 'Is there a quiet stream underneath the fluctuating affirmations and rejections of my little world? Is there a still point where my life is anchored and from which I can reach out with hope and courage and confidence?[4]

For some of us the journey towards finding that 'quiet stream' begins in tears but also with a burning passion to find a better way to live and by God's grace to discover an incredible truth: *nothing I do can make God love me more and nothing I do can make God love me less. There is nothing to prove.*

CHAPTER FOUR

TOMORROW BELONGS TO
THE FAILURES

One day our Sunday School teacher asked that the following week we bring an object to class that we could all discuss. All ten of us brought something, but I can remember three in particular. Peter Fisher took his hamster, at least he said it was a hamster; Mr Pendleton thought it looked distinctly like a rat and immediately locked it in the outside bathroom. Becky Adler took a cross made out of matches that her father had made when he was a prisoner of war in Japan. I took a large print that depicted Peter sinking in the storm because he took his eyes off Jesus; for as long as I could remember it had hung in my grandmother's house and I had exactly one hour to get it back before she missed it.

Mr Pendleton was a gracious man and he spent a while on each child's offering, drawing some spiritual lesson from every one, but he left my painting until last. Finally he held it up in front of the class.

'What do you notice about this painting?' he asked.

'Please, Mr Pendleton, the storm is very fierce,' said Tom Bradshaw.

'The disciples in the boat are dry,' offered Sheila Davenport.

And then, with a huge laugh, Clive Lewis said, 'Peter is up to his neck in water – he looks scared stiff!'

Mr Pendleton smiled, 'Well, all those comments are true and I'm sure Peter was afraid, but you have missed the most important point of all.' We puzzled for at least a few minutes, and then he said, 'How far do you think Peter is from the boat?'

We all guessed about six or seven metres.

'I agree,' said Mr Pendleton 'now what's special about that?'

'Please sir – he walked on the water!' blurted Tom.

'Yes,' said the old teacher. 'You see children, whenever you hear this story people always talk about Peter failing – taking his eyes off Jesus and sinking. And Clive is right, this painting shows him up to his neck in water, but it's only part of the story. The other part is that Peter walked on water. I know that he failed, and no doubt when he got back into the boat, the other disciples laughed at him. But, boys and girls, I think God would prefer you to have the courage to trust him even if you fail a little, than to never take a risk for him at all.'

And then he said something which will never get on one of those inspirational posters that you can hang in offices to motivate the staff, but I am convinced the old boy was right; he said, 'Tomorrow belongs to the failures.'

I will never forget the day it happened. My wife, Dianne, describes it like this:

> It was in so many ways a perfect morning. I had just woken and the sun was streaming into the room. I had a lovely home, a good marriage, and two beautiful children. The only problem was I had just turned to my husband and whispered, 'I don't think I can cope anymore.' But things like this didn't happen to people like me; and in any event I couldn't let them happen. I had a little girl who needed me and a brand new baby, and I had a real faith in God. People like me didn't crack up – did they?

I remember Dianne saying, 'I can't take Katie to school today' as though it were yesterday. I got up from bed and prepared Katie's breakfast, before dropping her off at nursery school. I can't remember whether or not I thought this was going to be just a bad day, but, if I did, I was wrong. Something had affected Dianne's immune system, causing her to sink into depression; whatever was going on in her life was not going to be solved overnight.

As the weeks turned into months I became more and more frustrated. I was, by now, a senior partner in a growing law practice, in demand as a speaker and up to my eyes in church leadership responsibilities. But the hardest thing of all was that I had no control over the circumstances that had suddenly hit our lives. In almost every other area of my life people came to me for help; I was the man who could make it happen, the person who could usually get the job done, the one you could rely on. But at home I was helpless. Worse still the emotional aspect as to what was happening to Dianne made it harder for some to sympathise. I got advice on how to be harder/softer/loving/tough. But nothing I did or didn't do made any difference. Dianne was ill.

I remember one night a leader from our church came to see me; he is a man with a big heart. I had just put the children to bed; Dianne was asleep upstairs. We talked for hours and then knelt in the darkness and prayed together. Suddenly I felt my shoulders begin to shake and I sobbed uncontrollably; none of the old resources worked in this situation. If I was wealthy I wasn't wealthy enough, if it was power I didn't have enough of it. I could only look up and ask God in his mercy to help us.

There is an old hymn which has these lines in it:

When we reach the end of our hoarded resources
Our Father's full giving has only begun.[1]

I have learned that it is necessary in the life of the kingdom to get to the end of those hoarded resources. These are the store of things on which we base our security. It could be our money, our talent, our position, our reputation. So long as we are relying on them we can achieve very little of lasting value. But there comes a time when we feel utter weakness, even failure, and at that moment we unleash a power so great it can over-whelm us. Jesus put it like this: 'Without me you can do nothing.'[2]

Those words do not mean that nothing is achieved. It

is, unfortunately, possible to get a lot done without the presence or power of Jesus. We can organise meetings, build sanctuaries and write books without him. It means nothing of value – nothing that lasts forever – gets done. But it is not the way of the kingdom. And it is for this reason that time and time again the Bible shows us the power not of success . . . but of failure.

Let's take a vote. We have a hundred people in a room. Who is your favourite disciple? John gets fifteen because Jesus loved him especially; Andrew gets four because, although often in the background, he was always bringing people to Jesus; Thaddeus gets one because there is always somebody just dying to show you how clever they are; but Peter gets eighty. Why? . . . Because he failed. We love Peter because he reminds us of ourselves.

There's no doubt that one of the most significant events in Peter's life was the subject of my grandmother's painting that we discussed in class that day. I don't suppose he ever forgot shouting through the storm, 'Lord, I want to walk on the water with you!' The word that came back to him, carried on the wind, must have chilled his heart; Jesus said, 'Come!' and Peter climbed over the gunwale of the boat and into the darkness.

It's true that he sank, but Mr Pendleton was right: *Peter walked on water.*

The critics will always be there. They will be sitting in the boat, perfectly dry and full of good advice as to how you got it wrong. But tomorrow belongs to those who are prepared to fail.

It was not long after the incident on Lake Galilee,

that Peter found himself in the big city – Jerusalem itself. It was just before dawn when it happened and the memory of two events never left him. The first was the sound of the cock crowing and the second was the look in the eyes of Jesus as he turned to him.[3] At least in Peter's defence, we can say that he wouldn't have seen those eyes unless *he* had been looking at Jesus, but this was the very lowest point in his life. Days before he had vowed to die with him; now, before sun-up, he was already on his third denial. Another of the disciples was to die that morning by his own hand – I wonder what kept Peter from doing the same? It may have been the conversation he had with the carpenter the night before. Jesus said, 'Simon, Simon (Peter's old name), Satan has asked to sift you as wheat. But I have prayed for you, Simon, that your faith may not fail.'[4]

As Peter thought about that it must have struck him that there is hope beyond failure – the hope of strength beyond weakness. He didn't have to wait too long to discover the truth of this. The Sanhedrin was the most powerful court in the whole of Israel and when the young fisherman stood to address it and make his defence you would have found it hard to recognise the man who had denied the faith to a servant girl. He did not seem like Peter the denier when, refusing to stay quiet about the message of the risen Christ, he said, 'We cannot help speaking about what we have seen and heard.'[5]

And I have no doubt that Peter would occasionally come across a man or woman who would whisper to him in the market place, 'Yesterday I denied the Master.'

And then they would hear some of the sweetest words we can ever hear from another human being: 'Me too.'

'You?' they would stutter. 'You denied him also?'

And Peter would again relate how God uses not the successful but the weak; he has plans for the failures.

Shortly after Dianne became ill she said to me that because she wasn't well enough to go to church, she would like to start a small Bible study in our home. We called it 'the strugglers group.' It was for those who were spiritual waifs and strays, those on the edge. Some had no faith, others had lost the faith they once held dear. We seemed a strange duo to meet the needs of such people. All we had to offer was our weakness. I remember saying to one particularly bright social worker who was not a Christian, 'I'm sorry you haven't got a better example of Christianity to look at – we're going through a tough time at the moment.'

One night some months later this person left our home in a particularly difficult mood. The evening had not gone well; we had tried to share our faith as well as we could but she, in particular, was very negative. I said to Dianne, 'I doubt if Gill will ever find faith in Christ.' At one o'clock in the morning my telephone rang. It was her:

'He has met me,' she said.

'What happened?' I asked.

'After I left,' she replied, 'I drove home across the mountains and suddenly I felt tremendous love and forgiveness to some people who had hurt me badly. He met me! My heart is physically hurting. Will it be like this tomorrow?'

I remember saying, 'I don't know. It's never happened to me like that, but you are very privileged. He has met you in a special way.'

It was just the first fruits of a great harvest from that group. We saw people find faith for the first time, others rediscover a relationship with God they thought had gone forever. Many of those who came are now in leadership roles themselves. What had been born in weakness was operating in a power I had never seen before.

You may be a great preacher, but be careful your gift does not get in the way of God moving in power. It would be better for you to stutter words that he wanted you to say, than to preach your best sermon in your own strength. You may be wealthy; it is a great responsibility. You must come to the point where you realise that God does not need your money. He says, 'Every animal of the forest is mine, and the cattle on a thousand hills . . . If I were hungry I would not tell you.'[6] It is your privilege to use what you have in his kingdom. And you must lay down the sense of control that wealth brings for it will ruin you. You may be a great organiser – but spend time listening, as well as doing. Have God bring you to the place where you would rather organise a tea-party that he wants, than arrange an international convention that a committee has dreamt up.

There is a very moving account at the beginning of Luke's Gospel.[7] Joseph and Mary had taken the boy Jesus, aged twelve, from the north down to Jerusalem to celebrate Passover. On the way back they suddenly realise that he is not with them and they begin to retrace their steps to find him. The Authorised Version of the Bible puts it very powerfully, 'But they, supposing him to have been in the company, went a day's journey . . . And when they found him not, they turned back again to Jerusalem, seeking him.'[8]

It can happen to us so easily in our careers, our ambitions and our church activities. We blast ahead, relying on our gifts, our resources, and all seems to be well. But we have gone on wrongly assuming that Jesus was with us. It is truly frightening to consider what can be achieved without God being with us and too scary for words to think about what it all adds up to: *nothing*.

If we go on but don't realise that Jesus is not with us, one of two things normally happens. Sometimes God causes us to go through an experience that makes us feel again our need of him. I am sure that I would not be writing this book now if it were not for the fact of Dianne's illness all those years ago. The other possibility is we never know – we are too concerned with ourselves, with our success, with the next project, with all we must achieve, to realise that actually *we are on our own*.

It is true that nothing succeeds like success. We live in a society that loves winners. Almost every day we receive junk mail that promises to make us successful; there are seminars, books and videos that promise to help us reach that goal. The media worships at the altars of those who have made it and we drool at their lifestyles. Nobody is ever going to write a best-seller called *How to Fail – Ten Steps to Ensure You Don't Make*

It and yet there is often a strange power at the heart of failure which can hold the key to greater success than we have ever dreamt of.

Real success belongs to those who suffer setbacks and somehow begin again, who experience crushing defeat and yet in that very moment learn lessons that sow the seeds of triumph; it belongs to those who learn in their weakness to draw on wells of strength they hardly knew existed.

The world may admire success – and I can understand that – but its aim is too low. Tomorrow belongs to the failures.

CHAPTER FIVE

WHEN YOU PLAY TO YOUR STRENGTHS THE GIANTS FALL FASTER

When I was seven years old I was bullied at school. John Thatchell used to wait for me every evening and chase me all the way home. I would hammer on our front door begging my mother to answer it quickly before the full weight of the muscle-bound ten-year-old descended on me.

And I owe it to John Thatchell that I can still recall almost word for word the way that Miss Lamarque used to tell my favourite story: David and Goliath. In fact it's not hard to understand why this is number one for so many children: because every child knows a bully, the story of the humbling of the giant is every child's dream. When we are small we don't understand that 'whose height was six cubits' means just about three metres; to us this is a bully the size of the Empire State Building. And of course I had heard it many times, and I knew the end, but I can still remember being scared as David picked five

57

smooth stones from the brook that day. What if five weren't enough?

And the story was scary. Imagine a seven-year-old listening to the threats of the giant: 'I will give your flesh to the birds of the air and the beasts of the field.' Don't miss, David!

But above all I can remember being mystified as to why David would not wear Saul's armour, and why, when he could have had the sword of the king, he trusted in a sling. But now, forty years on, I am not puzzled, and as I consider that account afresh I am challenged by its simple lesson: when you play to your strengths the giants fall faster.

The belief that he could do it had risen slowly in his heart.[1] True, it was a greater feat than he had ever accomplished, and the possibility of becoming a laughing stock and losing his life in the process was very real. And yet he still believed.

It was that belief that caused him to push his way through the soldiers, to the tent that stood in the middle of the encampment, and gave him the courage to actually speak the words, 'I want to see the king.'

The sergeant looked at him, smiled and said, 'Do you, lad? Now, who shall I say it is that wants an audience?'

David saw the smile leave the soldier's face, and he could hardly believe that he had said it, but, yes, the words had come out of his mouth . . . 'Tell him it's the giant-killer.'

And suddenly he, the shepherd boy, was face to

face with the most powerful man in the whole of Israel. The prepared speech stuck in his throat, and all he could remember later was mumbling about killing a lion that had threatened his sheep. He waited: the king smiled. It was hard to discern if he was impressed or just desperate, but the king agreed – the boy could fight Goliath.

And then it happened – an event so innocuous, so lacking in maliciousness that David did not at first realise the danger that almost cost him his life. King Saul said, 'You can do it, but I want you to wear this.' The King nodded to a slave nearby and it was carried in. It was unmistakable – David had seen it from a distance, he knew people that had almost died in the crush to touch it. It looked impregnable, as if any man who wore it would become immortal. As the slave held it high, the sun shining through the tent flap caught it and momentarily blinded David. He, the least of all his brothers, was to wear Saul's armour.

Of course, David said, 'yes'. He climbed into the huge metal gaiters, and waited patiently as the great iron breastplate was chained around his body. The helmet slid over his eyes and he had to hold it up to stop himself looking ridiculous. Two men lifted the sword and pressed it into his hands and it was all he could do to stop himself crying out at the pain of the weight that jarred his forearm. But finally it was done and he longed to be gone and get on with it. And, he would have been gone, but he realised that he simply couldn't move.

Every face was on him, and he lowered his head in

embarrassment. They knew. And then he saw it. One of the soldiers had ripped it from his belt as they had dressed him in the iron and it lay on the floor near the door of the tent. The leather that he had so painstakingly fashioned seemed old and listless compared to the gleam of the armour. And yet in a moment he knew what he must do. Later, as he remembered what he said to the king that day, he realised that it took at least as much courage to say it as to fight the giant, but it saved his life and, more importantly, allowed God to work.

'O king, there is no man in all of Israel I want to please more than you and no deed that means more to me than to kill the one who is pouring scorn on the God we serve, but I cannot wear your armour because I am not you. It may be hard for you to understand, but my real gift is in my sling. If you will just let me be me, I believe that God can do something that will amaze both of us.'

The king watched as the stone left the leather, and he hardly needed to follow its flight because it was all in the face of the boy – the faith, the gift . . . the freedom.

It's impossible to understand the heart of the story of David and Goliath without coming to terms with the concept of 'Saul's armour'. The principle is a very simple one but when we grasp it we find it to be life-changing. It is based on the fact that each of us has special gifts; these can be natural – like being good with numbers or sport – or spiritual, like preaching. The whole world may want to make us just like them, but when we operate within our own gifting, we not only see better results but, like David, improve our chances of achieving them without killing ourselves.

Let's say you have a gift of organising events. A large conference is coming up and somebody asks you to help. You have to raise some finance, plan the marketing and invite the speakers. You do it well. It's true it has taken the best part of six months and there have been hassles galore, but it's the day before the opening and it's ready to go.

And then somebody on the committee asks if you would mind saying a few words on the opening night. As they speak you can feel your heart-rate increase and you begin to sweat. You hate public speaking, and know that if you grant the request you will spend the next twenty-four hours worrying and practising and probably make a mess of it anyway. You know for sure that this is not a task you should undertake and so you say . . . *'Yes, of course I'd love to help!'*

It's important to realise what went on in that situation. At the very moment you said 'yes' you laid down your real gift. Like David's sling, it fell to the floor. That would have been bad enough, but you also climbed right into Saul's armour. You're no public speaker – and you know it – but you wanted to please somebody, you wanted to do your bit and perhaps there was even a little conceit at being asked. But beware, you are soon to be on top of a hill with a giant to kill and totally immobile!

Gift is a strange thing. It's very important that at some stages of our lives, and in order to discover our real gifts, we try things that we are pretty sure aren't our talents. There is many a man or woman whose primary gift is something they were once terrified of doing. That is not the same as spending *a lifetime* trying to do things that, for us, are 'Saul's armour'. And having discovered our gifts it's vital that so far as is possible *we play to our strengths*. The problem is that life is full of people who either want you to be just like them or seem determined to turn you into *their* idea of perfection. If you and I listen to them at least three things will happen: first, we'll become just like them – tearing around saying 'yes' to the whole world and losing our sanity in the bargain; next, we'll be so busy fulfilling other people's expectations of our life we'll never get round to finding out what God may have had planned for us; and lastly, not only do we never develop our God-given gifts, but we'll get in the way of others developing theirs.

But you could well say, 'You should come to my church. It's not exactly that we've got people rushing round grabbing other people's opportunities – we can't get anybody to do anything.' That may be true, but it's still no reason for you to do *everything*.

I wonder why we find it so difficult to say 'no' to those who ask us to help, even if this leads us into a life of crushing busyness in which we become totally ineffective. I can't help but believe part of the answer lies in a phrase that we don't hear much of today – 'the call of God' on our lives. When we have no real sense of that call, no certainty of what we are meant to be saying 'yes' to, it makes it hard to say 'no' to anything.

Somebody said to me years ago that Jesus achieved all he did in three short years because he did what his father told him to do. He had a clear understanding of what he was meant to be saying 'yes' to. The practical results in his life were that at times he knew it was right to say 'no.'

'Will you be our king?' – 'No.'[2]

'Will you settle this dispute between my brother and me?' – 'No.'[3]

'Will you come back to Capernaum?' – 'No. Let us go somewhere else . . . so I can preach there also.'[4]

Most of us are 'yes' people. We long to be needed and we crave to be liked, but we pay the price of never knowing the achievements and peace of those that have the security to play to their strengths – to listen to the call. Euripides put it like this: 'The same man cannot well be skilled in everything – each has his own special excellences.' Those 'special excellences' are vital. Paul gets to the heart of the issue when he says, 'If the whole body were an eye, where would the sense of hearing be?'[5]

It's never too late to change – but hurry! Quentin Crisp was right: 'It's no good running a pig farm badly for thirty years while saying, "Really I was meant to be a ballet dancer." By that time pigs will be your style.'

LET THE RABBITS RUN

Imagine there is a meadow. In that meadow there is a duck, a fish, an eagle, a squirrel and a rabbit. They decide they want to have a school so they can be clever just like people.

With the help of some grown-up animals, they come up with a curriculum they believe will make a well-rounded animal:

Running
Swimming
Tree-climbing
Jumping
and . . . flying.

On the first day of school Brer Rabbit combed his ears and went off to his running class. There he was a star. He ran to the top of the hill and back as fast as he could go, and oh, didn't it feel good.

The next class was swimming. When the rabbit smelt the chlorine he said, 'Wait a minute! Rabbits don't like to swim.'

The instructor said, 'Well you may not like it now, but five years from now you'll know it was a good thing for you.'

In the tree-climbing lesson a tree trunk was set at a 30 degree angle so all the animals had a chance to succeed. The little rabbit tried so hard he hurt his leg.

In the jumping lesson, the rabbit got along well. In the flying lesson, he had a problem. So the teacher gave him a psychological test and discovered he belonged in remedial flying.

The next morning he went on to his swimming lesson. The instructor said, 'Today we jump into the water.'

'Wait, wait. I talked to my parents about swimming. They didn't learn to swim. We don't like to get wet. I'd like to stop this course.'

The instructor said, 'You can't stop it now. At this point you have a choice: either you jump in or you fail.'

The rabbit jumped in. He panicked! He went

down once. He went down twice. Bubbles came up. The instructor saw that he was drowning and pulled him out. The other animals had never seen anything quite as funny as this wet rabbit who looked more like a rat without a tail, and so they chirped and jumped and barked and laughed at the rabbit. The rabbit was more humiliated than he had ever been in his life. He wanted desperately to get out of the lesson that day. He was glad when it was over.

He thought he would head for home, that his parents would understand and help him. When he arrived he said to his parents, 'I don't like school. I just want to be free.'

'If rabbits are going to get ahead, you have to get a diploma,' replied his parents.

The rabbit said, 'I don't want a diploma.'

The parents said, 'You're going to get a diploma whether you like it or not.'

They argued and finally the parents made the rabbit go to bed. In the morning the rabbit headed off for school with a slow hop. Then he remembered that the head teacher had said that any time he had a problem he should remember that the school counsellor's door is always open.

When he arrived at school he hopped up in the chair by the school counsellor and said, 'I don't like school.'

And the school counsellor said, 'Mmmm – tell me about it.'

And the rabbit did.

The school counsellor said, 'Rabbit, I hear you. I hear you say that you don't like school because you don't like swimming. I think I have diagnosed that correctly. Rabbit, I tell you what we'll do. You're doing well in running. I don't know why you need to work on running. I'll arrange it so you don't have to go running any more; you can have two periods of swimming instead.'

When the rabbit heard that he was very upset!

As the rabbit hopped out of the school coun- sellor's office he looked up and saw his friend the wise old owl, who cocked his head and said, 'Brer Rabbit, life doesn't have to be this way. We could have schools and businesses where people are allowed to concentrate on what they do well.'

Brer Rabbit was inspired. He thought that when he graduated, he would start a business where the rabbits would do nothing but run, the squirrels could just climb trees, and the fish could just swim. As he disappeared into the meadow, he sighed softly to himself and said, 'Oh my, what a great place that would be.'[6]

When we are allowed to use the special gifts that God has given us, life not only becomes more fulfilling but more effective. Other people's armour may look good, but when we operate within our own gifting we make a remarkable discovery: *the giants fall faster.*

CHAPTER SIX

DON'T SPEND YOUR LIFE WISHING YOU COULD HAVE DONE MORE

When I was a boy I used to believe that Sunday School teachers were all made somewhere special. First they were all so old and yet still alive. I was later told that some were as old as forty. But it wasn't just their age; God seemed to have given them strange features with which to delight small children. Mr Manley had eyebrows that looked like butterflies. If you made him cross his anger rose in stages. First he would go very red, and then his forehead would begin to shake, and if you were very fortunate you could almost make the butterflies take off.

I can't remember all his lessons but one is graven into my very being. The previous week he had asked our parents not to prepare us lunch the following Sunday but instead to make sandwiches which we should bring untouched to Sunday School. We came clutching our food.

The lesson started. It had gone on for ten minutes when Arthur Jenkins said, 'Please sir, can we eat our sandwiches?'

'Not yet,' replied the butterfly man. *Various requests by increasingly hungry children were refused until with fifteen minutes to go the old boy said, 'Now what if I asked you to give your sandwiches away?' We all gasped. He smiled, 'No, I won't ask you to give your lunch to Jesus today, but eat it quickly and I'll tell you about a small boy who did just that.'*

When Mr Manley began the story of the feeding of the five thousand he asked us to close our eyes and imagine. 'Imagine a hill that reaches down to the sea of Galilee, imagine you can smell the grass, and imagine you can see and hear the crowd that has gathered to hear the young carpenter that day.' I imagined. My Sunday School teacher had taken a boy who had never been further than twenty miles from his home, to the heart of the middle east, and introduced him to another boy who gave his lunch away.

But he was about to introduce me to more than that. He was to illustrate a principle that I have seen operate in all kinds of situations: when we stop worrying about what we can't achieve and, instead, do what we can, God can multiply our efforts beyond our wildest dreams.

When I was fifteen years old I wanted to be a rock and roll singer. I ended up as a senior partner in a law practice, and later as executive director of a national charity, but my heart then was in being able to master 'Johnny B. Goode' with three chords and a guitar that kept tune worse than me. Even now, sometimes, in the quiet of the early morning darkness, I consider all I am involved in and wonder if I would trade it all to walk onto the stage at Las Vegas and take my bow. Elvis was my hero. I had developed the art of lifting my top lip in that half sneer, half smile of his that I was convinced drove girls to distraction. I had an Elvis hairstyle, walked liked Elvis, talked like Elvis and sang like me.

And one day as I strode down my street humming 'Blue suede shoes' a man from our church approached me and asked if I'd like to do a Bible study once a week with him. He told me places were limited – apparently there were to be just two teenagers in his class. The boy whose life ambition was to climb into a gold lamé suit said 'yes.' Some time, deep in eternity, I will discover why I said 'yes' that day, but when I was fifteen years old – smoking, sneaking off to dances, and dreaming of stardom – I began a weekly Bible study.

He and his wife were poor but no poorer than we were; like us they did not own a house or a car, they shared a bathroom with the people upstairs. He had no qualifications and an ordinary job at which he worked hard to make ends meet. The course that we studied together had not exactly been written for a boy who wanted to make it to Las Vegas, but I never missed an evening.

He was a brilliant psychologist. We would study the Bible for thirty minutes, and then he would produce two pieces of hardboard which he would lay across the dining table, and hey presto – table tennis! But never before had the game been played in such a fashion. The small makeshift table filled the room, and we would play our shots with our hands tight to our chests. If the ball went under the table it was a five-minute job to retrieve it.

And after table tennis we would walk to the fish and chip shop together. By the time we got back the vinegar was seeping through the wrappings and his wife had the tea brewing. We loved those evenings. Don't tell me we loved them because in those far-off days teenagers were simple and easy to please. No, we went because this couple made us feel special. It was fun, and at times stretching, but not in a school way, and we felt as though we were *somebody*.

One night after a year of study he said to me, 'I want to see if you could learn to speak in public.' He took an old flannelgraph from a cupboard. For the uninitiated I should explain: it was a sheet of felt on which a scene had been printed – in this case of a hillside. The cardboard box that lay next to it contained all the equipment needed to tell the parable of the prodigal son – cut-outs of pigs, son, father and elder brother. The characters stuck to the felt and you put them on, or removed them, as you told the story.

It took months of practice. There were moments when it seemed certain that a career in public speaking was not likely; I remember one dark moment when I managed to get the old father in the sty and had a pig looking down the road waiting for his son to come home. But I got there eventually and one day he said to me, 'You're ready to take a children's meeting at church.'

Twenty years later I rang him from Vienna. The next day I was a keynote speaker, addressing a thousand lawyers at an international law conference. I said, 'You taught me to do it – it is because of you.' Since the start of Care for the Family I speak to him more often. I say to him, 'I've passed some of the skills you taught me on to others. Last night we spoke to thousands of people, or on this television programme or that radio station. We are reaching millions with a message that can revolutionise lives. You started it!'

So often we feel we have so little to offer. We look at society today, we perhaps mourn at the state of the church, we see men and women of great ability in prominent roles and say in our hearts, 'Thank goodness they are doing it – I have nothing to offer.' But that is always wrong. In fact it is almost sinful. It was Abraham Lincoln who said, 'God loves ordinary people – he made so many of them.' And the story of the Bible is of God using those who so often felt they had little to give – to change the world. 'But God chose the foolish things of the world to shame the wise; God chose the weak things of the world to shame the strong. He chose the lowly things . . . so that no one may boast before him.'[1]

I wonder how the young boy felt when the idea first crossed his mind. He had sat engrossed as the carpenter taught. Occasionally he would look around at the vast crowd sat on the hillside overlooking Galilee. And then he realised something was wrong. He had seen James whisper something into the Teacher's ear and then look crestfallen at whatever reply he had received. He could see the disciples arguing among themselves. He heard one of them say, 'A year's pay would not feed all these.' So that was it. The people were hungry, the teacher had told them to feed the crowd – but they had nothing.

And then the thought had risen in his heart. He began to get up, and practically fell again, his legs had all but gone to sleep. But soon he was pushing his way through the crowd, 'Excuse me, I have to get this to the Master.' And it was then he heard the voice in his heart, 'Who do you think you are? Sit down now before you embarrass yourself. That's Peter and John out there, do you think you know better than them? You're just a boy – forget your wild plans.'

He would have sat down that very moment – except he knew that if he did he would regret it even when he was an old man – and suddenly he was there, face to face with Andrew. 'It's just my lunch – my mother made it – a few fish and a little bread. If he wants it he can have it.'

He would never forget what he saw that day on the hillside at Galilee. The Master opened the cloth around his food and took out the bread, then the fish. He saw the hands of the carpenter hold them high above the crowd and call down the blessing of God. And then his lunch – the food his mother had prepared – was being broken to the crowd. When he was old he would tell the story to his grandchildren.[2]

Our church has a programme to help those who are homeless. Each week people bring food and clothing and, perhaps even more importantly, a sense of dignity to those that few others want to touch. Some years ago a mother in the church began to help. I have never heard her speak from the platform, she is often silent in house-group Bible studies, she has felt in the past she had little to give. The other night I discovered by accident that near to Christmas she had gone back into the city centre late one night to find a man whom she had noticed had no buttons on his coat. She sat beneath an arch and she sewed buttons on the jacket of the man who smelt, and who was cold. I have no doubt that there were many things that she felt she could not do but a man's life was touched that night because she did what she could.

Some years ago I was speaking at a conference in Belfast, Northern Ireland; I had been talking about the feeding of the five thousand, and in particular the young boy who gave his lunch away to the Master. I had urged each of us to discover something we could do for the kingdom, no matter how small, and to do it with all our heart. A woman came up to me after the event and told me the story of her granddaughter. The child was five years old and one day said to her mother, 'Mum, when is Jesus coming to our village?'

The mother was taken aback, 'Darling,' she said, 'he is always with us.'

The child replied, 'I know that, but when is he coming to our village?'

The mother pulled the child to her and asked, 'Why is this so important to you?'

'Well,' said the little girl, 'they have been telling me about him in Sunday School and all the things he did. I've saved my pocket money and I've got enough to buy five loaves of bread and two fish. If I could just get them to Jesus – he could feed the world.'

Don't spend your life wishing you could have done more – do today the small thing you can. And when you plant that seed you never know where it will end. After all, your Father is the gardener.

CHAPTER SEVEN

I WAS MEANT TO PARTY
WITH MY ENEMIES

*The highlight of our year was the Sunday School anniversary.
Every class would perform a short piece of drama or music for
the benefit of the invited parents. It seemed at times that we
practised these renderings all year. I am sure it was not the case,
but it seemed there was an incredible sense of competition among
the teachers as to which class would thrill the audience with its
innovations, move the parents to tears or, by dint of its amazing
choreography, have the whole church cheering. If there was such
a sense of competition it was not the fault of the church
authorities, for there were no winners or losers — except that
every child knew which class had come out on top and which
needed to fire the scriptwriter.*

*The pressure was intense. I have seen very together five-
year-olds — who have managed to hold down a preschool
playgroup, a reading class, and ballet — dissolve into tears because
they missed a cue or fumbled a line of poetry.*

But one year there was a slightly different focus. One bright Sunday School teacher had enlisted the help of all the other teachers and they appeared on stage as the disciples discussing which of them was the greatest. It's true that there was a little poetic licence but the drama was compelling:

Peter said, 'It must be me — I am the rock.'

John replied, 'But I am the one he loves especially.'

Matthew butted in, 'I'm a financier — new organisations need people like me.'

Judas would interrupt, 'I'm the treasurer. In two thousand years' time people will discover how powerful church treasurers are.'

And then Thaddaeus would speak, 'I'm Thaddaeus.'

It would be left to Peter to put him straight, 'Look, Thaddaeus, you're a valuable member of the team but nobody has ever heard of you. In two thousand years' time, when people try to remember all the disciples' names, it's yours they will forget. Thaddaeus, you are going to lose points for quiz teams.'

As you can imagine, the argument got pretty heated until, way over in the wings, a child began to read a passage from Mark's Gospel: 'Sitting down, Jesus called the Twelve and said, "If anyone wants to be first, he must be the servant of all." He took a little child and had him stand among them.'

And as the child read the passage, the teachers' arguments on stage got quieter until there was complete silence. Finally, the teachers were all standing to one side while centre-stage was a child, but not one of the children who normally got one of the leading roles, not one of the 'stars'. The audience were silent for what seemed an age as it mused over this living parable of the way God sees things. Then somebody in the audience began to clap; others joined in until it became the loudest applause I had ever heard in that little church. As I look back now I imagine that heaven itself was applauding.

———

Within twenty-four hours he would be dead and buried. It was probably a Thursday evening – Passover evening – and he had just a few hours left with his friends before those determined to kill him came for him. The room was prepared and now they could eat the sacred meal together.[1] And it was then, just as everything seemed ready, that it happened; the disciples realised there was no servant to wash their feet. Washing feet before dinner in the culture of the first century wasn't just tradition – it made for a sweeter atmosphere all around. But there was no one to do it. No one who would bend and wash away the dust and the dirt. They looked at one another for a while. In fairness things were pretty tense anyway; they had only just had an argument as to which of them was the greatest, so they weren't falling over themselves to do the servant's job.

And it was at that moment, as they were sitting petulantly, that they saw him rise from his seat, take a towel, and begin the task. James can remember what it felt like to have the Master rub away the dirt, and dry his feet. He felt ashamed and somehow humiliated, as if he should have known better. Peter took it worst of all. He never did anything by halves and simply refused to let Jesus wash his feet. But with tears and blushes the job was finally done.

They watched him take his seat again, and just knew that he was going to say something they would never forget, 'Now that I, your Lord and Teacher, have washed your feet, you should also wash one another's feet.[2] As I have loved you, so you must love one another.'[3]

There must have been so many issues that he could have brought to their hearts and minds on that last night but he chose this one. *He wanted them to love each other.* This was no easy task. In that group was Matthew who had collected taxes for the occupying forces of the Romans and at table with him was Simon the Zealot who hated the very sight of the Roman eagle. Judas was there, and James and John who had just revealed their personal ambitions for glory and said to the Master, 'When you come into your kingdom can I sit on your right hand and my brother on your left?' But he called them and us to love; to love those that hurt us, oppose us, plot our downfall; even to love our enemies. This matters to God more than whether we build the church extension, use modern songs or the old green hymn-book, sit sombrely in church or swing from the chandeliers, get to all the meetings, or have a fish badge on the back of our car.

He wants us to love each other.

Now here is a very strange thing. You can travel the length and breadth of this country and attend churches of all kinds. Your mind will be blown by the deadness of some and the life of others. You will experience beautiful liturgy, imaginative modern worship, and programmes enough to make you tired just listening to the notices. If you 'church-hop' you will at times believe that you have truly found the place 'just for you'. You say to friends, 'I know it's not perfect.' But in your heart you think it is. And that glorious state may last for a couple of years and then it will begin to dawn on you that never mind loving each other, some of the members actually hate each other.

You begin to hear murmurings of discontent. Classic comments are, 'I only care for the good of this church,' or 'I have been here from the beginning.' (The speaker is not claiming eternal status, just that they were on the very first building committee.) You start to notice that annual church meetings have the flavour of cup-ties. It's true that the opposing teams do not actually wear different colours but they do sit together in the stadium and they do predictably roar their approval or boo according to how their team is doing.

And then you realise something that at first you find hard to believe: that although these people have a manifesto of things they want to change – the worship, the teaching, the leaders, the youth leader, or the piano – actually those issues are not at the core of the problem. If all those things were sorted out immediately they would at once move on to something else. No, the real issue is relationships. And it is a tragedy.

It is a tragedy because it may well be that when we get to heaven we will discover that it wasn't of eternal consequence whether we met in a mega-church or a fifty-seater chapel; that actually God enjoyed worship equally as well sung from an overhead projector as a hymn-book; and heaven was never really holding its breath over whether we would take out the old pulpit and put in a full lighting rig. But if we do not strive for unity in our churches it is impossible that we will not feel ashamed when we meet him. This matters to him.

Over the past few years I have been presenting a seminar series on the issue of stress management. As I have talked with people after the event, or read the 'hurt mail' that comes into our office, I have become more and more convinced that the lives many of us lead as Christians are in fact more stressful than those of people outside the church. Now this would be acceptable if the kind of stress we are facing came out of our stand for the faith. Jesus warned his followers that discipleship was anything but an easy option. The problem is that many of us don't get near that kind of stress because we are too busy with a different kind – the kind that the Christian community imposes on itself. The church itself is becoming the greatest stress factor in the lives of many who are members.

You may have heard of the minister who was last to leave the church after a particularly difficult deacons' meeting. It was late and as he walked across the car park it was deserted save for his vehicle and an empty cola can which he kicked with sheer frustration. As he did so a genie came out and explained that the kick had freed him and the minister could have any wish he wanted. The genie explained, however, that he was only a junior genie and the wish ought not to be too difficult.

The minister thought a moment: he had so many needs – finance at home, a new car, a roof that needed mending, to name but a few – but finally the selfless part of him rose to the top and he heard himself say, 'An end to all war and violence forever.'

The genie looked stunned and said, 'I told you I was only a junior genie. Could you try me with something easier?'

'Oh, very well,' said the minister, 'could you make the people in the diaconate a little more amenable and not quite so difficult?'

The genie hesitated and said, 'Would you mind very much if we go back to your original wish?'

'People stress' is killing us; we are burning *one another* out. Rather than demonstrating the mutual support and encouragement we need if we are to reach a broken world, many of us are consumed with battles within the fellowship. You may say, 'But you don't know what difficult people we have in our church.' The truth is that we all have difficult people in our lives. You may think that in your church you have the most difficult person in the world, but you don't. There are difficult people in other churches that would make yours look like long-lost friends.

But difficult people need difficult issues to keep them going, and here again your church doesn't have the monopoly. A leading contender in this department is normally the music. This could be too loud, too modern or too ancient. Running a close second to the style of worship will be the teaching; this can be too deep, too shallow, or too long. Other issues will be the youth work, the building and, of course, the style of leadership.

It will be a great stress reliever if we can learn to live with our difficult people. A nineteenth-century railway company once realised that it was always the last carriage on the train that was involved in accidents; so they decided to remove it. Difficult people in church life are like that. You dream of the day they will leave. One day they do and you look forward to a time of unsullied bliss. But almost as soon as their feet are out of the door others rise up to take their place. These new ones are more difficult than the old ones dreamt of being – seemingly trained by watching their predecessors. It is not always possible, but if we can we should try to live with the ones we've got; after all, in their eyes, we're probably difficult too.

However, the issue is deeper than this and there are some important considerations in local church life that we ignore at our peril. One is that the local church is not the playground. In the playground there are un-written rules. The first of these is that you play with your friends. Church is not meant to be that way. Jesus gave a hint of it when he talked about not just inviting your friends to your parties. The world does that. You can have a room full of like-minded people having fun together in any old club in the world. But life in God's kingdom should be different; this kingdom is about enemies joining in, going 'extra miles' and the royal law of love. What it is not about is a group of like-minded people feeding each other's discontent. The urgency of getting this right comes over powerfully in the letter Paul wrote to the Christians at Corinth:

> I have a serious concern to bring up with you, my friends, using the authority of Jesus our Master. I'll put it as urgently as I can. You *must* get along with each other. You must learn to be considerate of one another, cultivating a life in common . . . You're fighting among yourselves . . . You're all picking sides, going around saying, 'I'm on Paul's side,' or 'I'm for Apollos,' or 'Peter is my man,' or 'I'm in the Messiah group.' I ask you, 'Has the Messiah been chopped up in little pieces so we can each have a relic all our own?'[4]

I have a hunch that when we stand before him we will find that God was not as concerned about the music, the building or even the style of teaching as we were. What he will want to know is how much we sweated, bled and struggled, what price we paid as peacemakers that the prayer of his Son that 'they may be one'[5] might be fulfilled on earth.

In the playground we have the wonderful sanction that if things don't work out as we want, we can always take our ball home. And in church if we are upset then we can stop giving financially, or threaten some other sanction, but we would do well to remember that is not how God normally deals with us. If God withdrew his favour from us the second we ceased to please him we would find that our very next breath was in danger.

Our money and our gifts are not ours to barter with – they belong to him.

We may decide to leave the church, and I fully understand that some do it after years of heart-searching and honestly believing there is no alternative; it may be that sometimes there is no other way, but it is a massive step. I am staggered at the speed at which some people move from church to church because they are unhappy. You rarely find they have moved because they suspect heresy; it is far more likely that this new church doesn't suit them any longer. Once embarked upon it is a weary road they have chosen for they are destined to *never* find their perfect church and to drive others to despair trying to please them.

In the playground there is little forgiveness. You can lose your status as 'best friend' by offering the bag of sweets to the wrong person. But church should be different. It is not a surprise to God that Christians have such a hard time getting on with each other. That is the very reason why the ministry of Jesus and the letters of the New Testament are continually talking about putting things right with people, forgetting the past, not nursing our hurts – in short, about forgiveness. When we cannot or will not strive for forgiveness, we become bitter. Forgiveness is at the heart of God's kingdom. This is not a matter of having all our hurts sorted out so that we feel good about them; it is rather the principle of letting go of them, remembering that they are nothing compared to the hurt we bring to God.

It's time to be honest. We are all difficult in some way.

We can all be bruised or offended and each of us has an inalienable belief in our own 'rightness'. But if we do not strive to be peacemakers it is not different music we need, or a better youth leader, or a new building or even deeper teaching. Our need is for God to reveal to us how much we owe to him. This is not a matter of agreeing with each other, or going on holiday with people we can't stand. It's about striving, bleeding for unity. It's about laying down agendas that don't matter, letting go of personal hurts and ambitions, denying ourselves the warm satisfaction of gossip, and growing up spiritually.

When somebody hurts us we have several very natural reactions. First, we want to justify ourselves. We want to show that person was wrong in what they did to us. One way we achieve that is to gather around ourselves others who have also been hurt by the person that offended us. The next step is to share our mutual hurt. The final phase follows naturally; we gradually decimate the character of the 'guilty' person. But there is another of dealing with this situation. We say *nothing*. We do not share our hurt with others; instead we bring it to God. If there is any vindicating to do, we leave it to him. 'Blessing your enemies' does not mean they never have to answer for what they have done to you; it means they answer directly to God. He has said, 'Don't insist on getting even; that's not for you to do.' 'I'll do the judging,' says God. 'I'll take care of it.'

The local church is an awesome invention. It is not a mistake in the mind of God. When a church cares more about what matters to God than anything else, there is no end to what it can achieve – no matter what its type, style or denomination. We are a special people on a special mission and when we bring each other down we make it hard for us to be effective. That's why James said,

> Don't bad-mouth each other, friends. It's God's Word, his Message, his Royal Rule, that takes a beating in that kind of talk. You're supposed to be honouring the Message, not writing graffiti all over it.[6]

We live in a broken world that is crying out for help. People have an ever-increasing belief that they are worthless; we have a growing sense of meaninglessness in society today and many experience poverty that shames us all. There are single parents to sustain, lonely people to comfort, families that are breaking up so fast it's taking our breath away and, above all, there are people, ordinary people, who need somebody to tell them about Christ. We simply do not have time to major on minors; the task is too great and too urgent.

I'm old enough to remember the 'cod war'. I should say that the name was deceptive. Never in the history of fishing have cod been so safe. And the reason was that the cod war was actually between the fishermen. They cut each other's nets and generally made life as difficult as possible for each other. In fact, if you were a piece of cod it was time to get your lilo out and enjoy the sun. Do we really think that those outside the church care about our petty squabbles, and does it no longer hurt us that God's name is tarnished by our divisions? Why have we found it so hard to believe that loving each other matters to God?

WALKING ONE NIGHT

Walking through the city late one night, I came upon a guy about to jump off a skyscraper. I said, 'Wait a minute, don't you believe in God?'

He said, 'I do believe in God.'

I said, 'Really? Are you a Christian or a Jew?'

He said, 'I'm a Christian.'

I said, 'Me too!' I said, 'Are you a Protestant or a Catholic?'

He said, 'A Protestant.'

I said, 'Really, what denomination?'

He said, 'Baptist.'

I said, 'Me too! Northern or Southern?'

He said, 'Northern.'

I said, 'Northern Conservative Baptist or Northern Liberal Baptist?'

He said, 'Northern Conservative Baptist.'

I said, 'Me too! Northern Conservative Reformed Baptist or Northern Conservative Fundamentalist Baptist?'

He said, 'Northern Conservative Fundamentalist Baptist.'

I said, 'Me too! Northern Conservative Fundamentalist Baptist Great Lakes Region or Northern Conservative Fundamentalist Baptist Eastern Region?'

He said, 'Northern Conservative Fundamentalist Baptist Great Lakes Region.'

I said, 'Me too! This is incredible! Northern

Conservative Fundamentalist Baptist Great Lakes
Region Council of 1879 or Northern Conservative
Fundamentalist Baptist Great Lakes Region
Council of 1912?'
   He said, 'Northern Conservative Fundamentalist
Baptist Great Lakes Region Council of 1912.'
   I said, 'Die, heretic!' and pushed him off.[7]

Last Sunday in a church somewhere near you, somebody was hurt. Even if that organisation has a super-
efficient church administrator, who logs every injury
on church premises in an accident book, the page for
that day will be blank. And yet, in spite of the fact that
no record exists of this event, the repercussions of it
will affect that church for the next decade. Because of
this event there will be small children who never get
to hear of the Sunday School, let alone attend it.
Because this thing occurred, there will be broken
families that never get help, and others for whom the
message of the faith remains a mystery – shrouded in
the fog of the church that stands in the heart of their
neighbourhood.

It is true that the act did not seem significant at the
time but it contained a seed that nobody saw hit the
ground that day. Over the coming months and years
that seed will grow in secret like a cancer and finally
pick its moment. When its fruit blossoms the poison it
contains will explode with devastating effect. Years later
people will ask, 'What happened to that congregation?'
but nobody will remember the event through which it
all began – an act that eventually paralysed that church,
then split it, and finally, as hell laughed loudly, spewed it

out all over the neighbourhood.

Well, what is this great event that happened last week in a church near you (perhaps *very* near)? I have painted the outcome of it in such cataclysmic terms that now, when I mention it, you won't believe me. But it is true: last Sunday somebody was offended, their feelings were hurt, they felt slighted in some way. It almost certainly wasn't as important as doctrine and perhaps it was something relatively insignificant. It just may have touched somebody in the area of their self-worth or ego; it was important to them.

The Bible assumes it will happen; when it comes to life in the local church it presupposes that we will hurt each other, disagree, fall out, and for that very reason whole chunks of it are dedicated to facing the person who has hurt us, telling them they have done so, forgiving, striving for peace, letting go of our petty hurts, and all for the utterly compelling reason that God has forgiven us.

But it is here that we meet a very great difficulty; it is a matter of great sadness. It is simply that many of us live in two worlds. In one of these worlds – our 'church world' – there are sermons. Those talks are full of teaching on forgiveness, grace, love and what it means to suffer for Jesus's sake. In that world, as well as sermons, there is what we call Christian service. This could be youth work, music, missions, projects for disabled people or house-group leadership. This is what we 'do'. And there are books in that world – books on holiness, prayer, tithing, forgiveness, and church planting.

But there is always, alongside that world, another place.

This is our 'inner world'. This is the part of us from which we run our lives. We were not aware of doing so but long ago we erected vast Chinese walls between the two worlds. If somebody preaches on giving sacrificially in the 'church world' we agree with them, but later when we look at our bank statement in the 'inner world' we find that it is untouched by any recent debit. We sing in the 'church world' of our desire to tell the world the message of the King, but when we glance into the 'inner world' we discover that our next-door neighbours have never been invited in for coffee.

And in the 'church world' we thank God that he has forgiven us, time and time again. In this world we acknowledge that very forgiveness as our only hope in eternity – that when we hurt him deeply our relation-ship can be restored. But the hurt last week will occur in the 'inner world'; in that part of our being which is untouched by the Spirit of God and his gentleness. And so we will deal with it as would anybody else. We will nurse it, and soon we will find others who themselves have been hurt by that person and we will share our experiences. And the bitterness and the anger and the hate will grow so that it is quite out of proportion to the original hurt. And one day we will get revenge. Oh, such a moment will be dressed up in religious language, but it will be common-or-garden hell at work.

And all would be well were it not for two things: the first is that God is the reader of people's hearts and can therefore look over the walls that separate our two worlds; the second is that we will meet him. The day will come faster than we think. Death will say, 'Now,' and we will stand before him. We will not be proud in that day over some of the battles that seem so vital now. And so while there is still time, let us lay down every personal agenda, let us be willing to 'spend and to be spent' for the sake of the kingdom, so that in that moment we will not be ashamed. And so a broken world can again look to its local church with hope.

THE PARABLE OF THE GEESE

Next autumn, when you see the geese heading south for the winter, flying along in a V-shaped formation, you might consider what science has discovered as to why they fly that way. As each bird flaps its wings it creates an uplift for the bird immediately following. By flying in a V-formation the whole flock adds at least 70 per cent more to its flying range than if each bird were flying on its own.

When a goose falls out of formation it suddenly feels the drag and resistance of trying to go it alone, and quickly gets back into formation to take advantage of the lifting power of the bird in front.

When the leading goose gets tired it rotates back in the wing and another goose flies point. It is sensible to take turns doing demanding jobs . . . whether with people or with geese flying south. Geese honk from behind to encourage those up front to keep up their speed.

When a goose gets sick, or is wounded by gunshot and falls out of formation, one or two of the other geese fall out with it and follow it down to lend help and protection. They stay with the fallen goose until it is able to fly or until it dies. Only then do they launch out on their own, or with another formation, to catch up with their group.

People who share a common direction and sense of community can get where they are going much more quickly and easily because they are travelling on the thrust of one another's efforts. If we have as much sense as a goose we will stay in formation with those who are headed the same way we are. If we have the sense of a goose, we will stand by each other when danger threatens or trouble comes.[8]

A PRAYER OF JESUS SHORTLY BEFORE HE DIED

Father the time has come. Glorify your son that your son may glorify you . . . I have revealed you to those whom you gave me . . . I will remain in the world no longer, but they are still in the world and I am coming to you. Holy Father, protect them by the power of your name – the name you gave me – so that they may be one as we are one . . . My prayer is not for them alone. I pray also for those who will believe in me through their message that all of them may be one . . . that the world may believe that you sent me.[9]

If you want to live a radical Christian life that will catch the attention of those who have no faith; if you want to belong to a church that no matter how large or small, will be a revolutionary force for good, there is a way it can be achieved but do not turn first to systems, meetings, or even church growth strategies: instead, party with your enemies.

CHAPTER EIGHT

SOMETIMES ANSWERS AREN'T
THE LAST WORD

It was a warm June day when our friend died. We had only just run onto the soccer field when it happened. Nobody tackled him, hit him or pushed him; Carl just died. He was running for a ball when suddenly he fell over. The game went on for several minutes before anybody realised that this was more than an effort to convince the referee he'd been fouled. We called an ambulance but it so happened that day there was a huge anti-government protest in our town and the paramedics were delayed getting to him.

The four of us sat outside the emergency room and waited. We saw nurses and doctors rushing along the corridors; they may have been late getting to the football field but now the whole world seemed involved in trying to save our friend. And then we saw Carl's parents. His mother was crying; his father, stern-faced, was practically dragging his wife along the corridor to the room where they were trying to save his son.

An hour later a doctor told us that Carl had died. An abnormality of the heart that had been undetected since birth, had ended the life of a boy who could curve a ball so the goal-keeper dived into thin air. To young minds it seemed such a waste, and so unfair.

That night as I sat at home with my parents there was a knock at our door. It was Carl's dad: he wanted to know what happened. He seemed angry and demanded to know in detail how his son had died. 'Did anybody strike him?' 'Did he cry out?' 'Could you have called for help more quickly?' I answered him as best I could, but even as I child I knew that Carl's father wanted the answer to a question that nobody on the face of the earth could give. He wanted to know why his son was dead.

When the kids filed into Sunday School the next day the normal naughtiness was gone: the class was red-eyed and sombre. I remember our teacher looking at us, sighing and putting aside the notes he had prepared for that week's lesson. He spoke slowly as if unsure of where he was going, almost feeling out each word: 'This week we will leave our study on the parables of Jesus. I want to take you instead to one of the oldest books in the whole Bible, and to a question that has bothered men and women for as long as life has existed: "Why does a good God allow suffering?" But before we start let's ask for God's help.'

I can't remember the exact words of my teacher's prayer that day, but I recall well the gist of what that old man asked of God: 'Heavenly Father, we are sad today and, if the truth be told, a little angry and confused. But we love you and we trust you. Please help us, as we study a little of the book of Job, to understand as much as we can about these deep questions and, even more important than that, help us to deal with what we can't understand. Amen.'

More than forty years have passed since that summer day when Carl died and the Sunday School lesson that followed it, but still my teacher's prayer echoes in my heart. 'Lord help me to deal with what I cannot understand . . .'

It was late on a cold February afternoon when I first walked alongside the railway track and under the arch that leads into the former concentration camp of Auschwitz. Less than sixty years ago that track carried cattle trucks with their cargoes of human life from all over Germany, Poland and France.

Those who came under the arch at Auschwitz had already suffered more than almost any man or woman can bear; many had travelled hundreds of miles with little water, no food and sharing the trucks with the corpses of loved ones who had died on the journey. It is difficult for us now, with the advantage of history, to believe that those people felt any sense of relief as they reached what we now call death camps, but they did. At last the journey was over, they had arrived, the future had to be better than the past. What more could their persecutors do to them?

The platform at which the trains used to stop is still there. To the right of the platform those that were fit and strong disembarked but those that were old or sick and the very young got off the train on the other side. And on the left, at the end of the platform were the buildings. They were told they were showers and were hustled towards them. As they went in soap was given out. To the right of the buildings was the crematorium.

As the war was coming to an end and just before the Russian army entered Auschwitz the commandant ordered that the buildings at the end of the platform be blown up, but they never quite managed it. And on that cold day, with the mist coming in across the camp, I stood in the remains of the gas chambers. As I tried to picture the memories the walls held, I imagined I could hear the screams of those who first sensed that it was gas and not water pouring down on them. I bent and picked up a piece of stone, something to remind me of the moment. But then, as I gazed down at the piece of brick in my hand, I let it fall. To take it seemed sacrilege; this was not a time for souvenirs, the suffering was too great. In my heart I searched for answers to the question 'Why?' But I was strangely comforted by the fact that none came.

When I was writing this chapter I showed the draft to a friend and colleague; she is one of the most gifted women I know, but she has known a lifetime of sickness. In her younger years she experienced depression that at times seemed to plunge her into a living hell. In more recent years she has had innumerable operations and on several occasions her life has hung in the balance. She is courageous beyond words and tells me it has not just been the excruciating pain that has brought her so low but the sheer frustration of having so much that she wants to do and yet spending much of her life feeling so very ill.

As she sat in my study and read she began to cry; first she sobbed quietly but then as she came to the end she cried uncontrollably. When she had composed herself she said, 'The love and support given to me by close friends and family over the years has been sent from heaven itself, but I have also spent a lifetime listening to Christians giving me answers as to why I have suffered. Some have said, "You must have offended God in some way." Others have offered, "If you had enough faith you could be well today." Some, trying to be kind, have suggested that God is trying to teach me something and I will be a better person because of my illness.'

And then she paused, and said through her tears, 'You have no idea what a release it is for me to read these words. What people don't understand is that answers are not always vital to those who suffer. I don't always have to know why. There are comforts deeper than explanations.'

Sometimes answers come too quickly, for there are moments in life when we should accept that we do not understand. Times when we observe the deep suffering of others may well come into that category. On 13 March 1996, just before 9.30 in the morning a gunman walked into the gymnasium of a primary school in Dunblane, Scotland and opened fire on the children and their teacher. Sixteen children and their teacher died that day; another twelve children and two teachers were injured.

Steve Chalke, who is both a Baptist minister and a television presenter, got a call from GMTV to fly to Dunblane to report on the situation. He was teamed up with Lorraine Kelly to co-present the bulletins. When he got there the cameras were already set up, but it was now dark and the temperature below freezing. He said that he and Lorraine stood frozen to the core, their hands so cold they could hardly hold the microphones. They would bring a short report and then, the second they were off-air, dive into a car which had been left with the engine running and heater at full blast, to try to thaw out before the next report.

Steve and Lorraine were in the front seats and the cameramen in the back. The radio was on and the announcer introduced a member of the clergy who was asked to comment on why God allowed such suffering. Steve says that the man gave a good, robust, textbook answer, but with little compassion, anguish or pain. After he had finished there was a long silence in the car. Finally, one of the cameramen, almost in tears, stretched over, turned the radio off and said, 'Crap.'

Steve said, 'I didn't disagree with the cleric's answer – everything he said had been entirely correct. It had just come at the wrong time, in the wrong place and in the wrong way.'

Just then it was time to go outside and back on air. As the red light flicked on the camera to show that people all over the country were now watching,

Lorraine Kelly turned to Steve and said, 'Steve, people are blaming God for what has happened, what do you say to that?'

Steve paused and then millions of people heard him say, 'That's all right; his shoulders are big enough.'

When Steve first told me what he had said my reaction was strange and I couldn't quite understand it. He had not defended God, he had not given any answers, he could easily have been misinterpreted; and yet it seemed to me that his answer not only honoured those who were suffering, but God himself. It was as if God was sharing their suffering; he was part of it.

I have discovered that very often those who are going through deep suffering do not always want answers. They want to know that if there is a God in heaven, he understands their pain. Those of us who have become familiar with the Gospel accounts of the last days of Jesus's life have a great difficulty in this area. We have become numb to the suffering he knew.

Today all over the world men and women will be tortured. As you read this, somebody is crying out in pain. Somewhere the modern equivalent of a crown of thorns is being forced on to a man's head. Somewhere, in a stinking cell, the words of Matthew's Gospel are being replayed today, 'They . . . took the staff and struck him on the head again and again.'[1]

And somewhere in our world today a woman is being betrayed by those she trusted. It may be the betrayal that will lead her to the executioner as it did for Jesus, or more likely it will be first noticed by the hotel receipt and the letter found in her husband's pocket as she searches for some keys. And I wonder, as she cries out in her pain, whether anybody will tell her that God understands betrayal.

And today there is somebody who, when it comes to the moment of greatest need, will be left alone by his friends. Oh, they will say kind things, and promise to call, but as he walks away from them he will know in his heart that he is, in truth, utterly alone. It was so when God walked the earth. It was not even the pain of Peter's denial, which came as no surprise, but rather the inevitability that finally they would all leave him. All the promises, all the affection, all the bravado, would come to nothing.

And then there is that agonising cry from the cross, 'My God, my God, why have you forsaken me?'[2] I have heard preachers trying to explain away that God-forsaken cry. But it cannot be explained away. It is mysterious, it is filled with pain, it does not easily succumb to answers.

I was once involved in a debate on the subject of 'Why does God allow suffering?' Halfway through, it was interrupted by a man in a wheelchair. He had cerebral palsy. He could not keep his head still, saliva ran down his chin, but he gestured that he wanted to say something. His speech was hard to decipher, and it took him a long time to communicate what was on his heart, but it was simple and he repeated it for us, 'People look at me and say, "Why?" I look up at heaven and say, "Why not?"'

The debate all but ground to a halt. We were now puzzled by a new phenomenon. It is that, so often, those at the heart of the suffering are not asking, 'Why?'

We need to walk humbly in this area. It is no shame to say, 'I don't really understand why your pain is so great, and why you, who are loving, have been so hurt.' But we can then add, 'God understands your pain and he is with you in it.' To those of us involved in the answers business, in having everything wrapped up and labelled, that doesn't seem much of a reply, but to those in the deepest pain, it often brings both comfort and hope.

In one of the oldest books in the Bible, Job searches for answers to suffering; he looks up to heaven and asks 'Why?' In one of the most dramatic renderings in the whole of literature God answers him.

Who is this that darkens my counsel with words
    without knowledge?
Brace yourself like a man; I will question you,
and you shall answer me.

Where were you when I laid the earth's foundations?
Tell me, if you understand.
Who marked off its dimensions? Surely you know.
On what were its footings set, or who laid its
    cornerstone?

Who shut up the sea behind doors when it burst forth
    from the womb,
when I said 'This is where your proud waves
    halt'?

Have you ever given orders to the morning or shown
   the dawn its place?
Have you journeyed into the springs of the sea or
   walked in the recesses of the deep?
Have the gates of death been shown to you?
Tell me, if you know all this.

Where does the light live?
And where does the darkness reside?
Do you know the path to their dwellings?
Surely you know, for you were already born!
You have lived so many years!

Can you bind the beautiful Pleiades?
Can you loose the cords of Orion?
Do you hunt the prey for the lioness?
Do you give the horse his strength?
Does the hawk take flight by your wisdom?
Does the eagle soar at your command and build his
   nest on high?

The Lord said to Job, 'Let him who accuses God
   answer him!'

*Then Job said, 'I put my hand over my mouth; I've
   said enough.'*[3]

There have been moments in my life when I have sat
by a hospital bed and cried with those who suffer. I
have stood by graves that claimed lives far too young,
and at times I have wept for my own pain. If at such
times there are 'whys' that I can comprehend then
whisper them to me. But you must also understand

that at such moments reasons will not be my deepest need. And if in silence you simply hold me and cry with me, I *will* be comforted.

Chapter Nine

You're not home yet

I can still remember almost word for the word many of the songs we sang in Sunday School. I'm sure that at the time I didn't appreciate all I was singing, but as I muse on those words now they come back to me with fresh insight.

It's winter, and although it's only half-past three in the afternoon it's already getting dark. Mr Wallace, the Sunday School superintendent, has switched on the large lights that hang from the centre of the church. Our individual classes are over and now the whole Sunday School gathers for a final hymn together. Mr Wallace announces, 'Number 124 in Golden Bells.' I know it before I look it up.

There's a friend for little children above the bright blue sky
A friend who never wearies, whose love will never die . . .

Most of us spend a lifetime looking for a friend like that.

'*Verse two!*' *says Mr Wallace, and a hundred kids begin singing not just about a friend, but a destination – 'There's a home for little children above the bright blue sky.'*

As a small boy of six I used to wonder what that home was like; it seemed so wonderful. Of course, as I got older there was no shortage of people who told me it only existed in my imagination. I never lost my belief in that place but it was not until I was in my forties that an event occurred which convinced me of its reality not only intellectually or theologically, but actually – in my heart. I'll tell you about that occasion a little later in this chapter. C.S. Lewis also grasped it as an adult and nowhere expressed it more wonderfully than in the closing words of his book for children, The Last Battle:

> For them it was only the beginning of the real story. All their life in this world . . . had only been the cover and title page: now at last they were beginning Chapter One of the Great Story which no one on earth has read: which goes on for ever and ever: in which every chapter is better than the one before.[1]

There is, tucked away at the heart of the Hebrew Old Testament, a fascinating book. Its name has been interpreted in several ways – 'teacher', 'professor' – but I like best 'philosopher'. I choose that particular word because the book of Ecclesiastes is always asking the question, 'Why?' It pushes us to consider the big questions of life and time and time again it does so by reminding us of the thing we do not want to hear: one day we will die.

In the early chapters of Ecclesiastes is a poem; the last line has in it the two great events of international life, 'A time for war and a time for peace,'[2] but the opening line has the two certainties of individual life, 'A time to be born and a time to die.'[3]

We don't like to talk about it; Os Guinness has called it 'the new pornography'. A hundred years ago it was sex that was taboo, but now in the number one slot is death. Some years ago I was at a party when the guests began to chat about their respective occupations. I noticed that one woman was very reticent. Later, when the other guests had moved away, she whispered in my ear, 'I'm an undertaker.' She had learned over the years that the phrase was, in every sense, a party stopper.

We live with death and see more of it, second-hand, that any other society that has ever existed. Every news bulletin brings us pictures of it – train crashes, air disasters, wars and famine. And yet, unlike previous generations, many of us are quite old ourselves before we actually see a dead person. I wonder if it is that which allows many of us to go through life juggling two ideas: the first is that intellectually we know we are going to die; the second whispers to us, 'Not you.'

Of course whole industries have risen to help us beat the odds. I am convinced that the battle against ageing is actually a battle against death. We do not want to grow old because we do not want to die. We do not wear the marks of age with pride as have other cultures; to us the wrinkles and the grey are a shame – a whisper of mortality. And so we can purchase 'ageing cream'. One poor man, untutored in the exact nature of this remedy, remarked to a friend who had been using it for months but whose face was still severely lined, 'Well, it seems to be working.'

But modern society is normally a little more sophisticated than that when it comes to pretending we can halt the march of time. When we are shown pictures of ageing actresses lounging across the centrefolds of magazines we do not give the game away, we do not talk of cosmetic surgery or makeovers or even old-fashioned corsets. No, we smile in admiration and say, 'She's good . . . for her age.'

The battle reaches its intensity when we have to declare our true age. The idea that women hate doing this more than men is a nonsense. I remember being with a company director whom I knew was fifty-six years old. When asked how old he was he replied, 'Middle aged.' He almost got away with it but a colleague leant over to him and whispered in his ear, 'Middle-aged? How many people do you know of a hundred-and-twelve?'

There comes a time when we do not want to get old. I think it occurs at twenty-four. Until then we tend to add time on. I was at a friend's house recently; they have two children. When asked his age, Simon told me he was five-and-a-half, whereas Emma declared proudly she was eleven-and-three-quarters. Those fractions matter to them. But when we hit twenty-four we say, 'Just gone twenty.'

Bob Hope was once interviewing an actress whom

he sensed wasn't quite as young as she made out. He said, 'Do you mind my asking how old you are?'

She replied, 'Approaching forty.'

Hope asked, 'From which direction?'

But it is all so understandable – the ageing process can be difficult to come to terms with. I read the other day that at your twenty-fifth school reunion you wear a name badge so that others will know who you are; at your fiftieth school reunion you wear a badge so *you* will know who you are!

It is very hard, and yet time and time again the Bible urges us to be real about the fact that we are going to die. We can so easily believe that we have such power; we can put a man or woman on the moon, we can move information at frightening speeds, we can give a person a new heart and yet what the old Jewish wise man said thousands of years ago is still true today, 'The length of our days is seventy years – or eighty, if we have the strength.'[4] And we are urged to 'number our days'.[5] That doesn't mean we can guarantee how long we have left to live. Rather, the principle of numbering our days means we acknowledge the brevity of this life. It urges us not to get too preoccupied with buildings or money or prestige because those things pass so quickly. The book of Ecclesiastes puts it like this, 'I hated all the things I had toiled for under the sun because I must leave them to the one who comes after me. And who knows whether he will be a wise man or a fool?'[6] Numbering our days does not mean we don't work hard, or try to achieve great things. It means we put those things in context, of the whole of life – friends, family, God.

111

All of this was impressed strongly on Dr James Dobson some years ago. He recounts an incident that occurred whilst he was at Los Angeles Children's Hospital.

One of my colleagues died during my last year at Children's Hospital, having served on our university medical faculty for more than twenty-five years. During his tenure as a professor, he had earned the respect and admiration of both professionals and patients, especially for his research findings and contributions to medical knowledge. This doctor had reached the pinnacle of success in his chosen field, and enjoyed the status and financial rewards that accompany such accomplishment. He had tasted every good thing, by the standards of the world.

At the next staff meeting following his death, a five-minute eulogy was read by a member of his department. Then the chairman invited the entire staff to stand, as is our custom in situations of this nature, for one minute of silence in memory of the fallen colleague. I have no idea what the other members of the staff contemplated during that sixty-second pause, but I can tell you what was going through my mind.

I was thinking, 'Lord, is this what it all comes down to? We sweat and worry and labour to achieve a place in life, to impress our fellow men with our competence. We take ourselves so seriously, overreacting to the insignificant events of each passing day. Then finally, even for the brightest among us, all these experiences fade into history, and our lives are summarised with a five-minute eulogy and sixty seconds of silence. It hardly seems worth the effort, Lord.'[7]

So long as we only think of this life, we will spend it stamping and kicking to preserve our hold on it – our possessions, our opinions, our ambitions. But at the very best we only get seventy years or so.

> Death lays its icy hand on Kings;
> Sceptre and crown
> Must tumble down
> And in the dust be equal made
> With the poor crooked scythe and spade.[8]

An Eastern monarch sent his wise men away to find a phrase that would fit every circumstance of life. They were gone for seven years but finally came back with it. You can write this phrase over buildings, circumstances, and our very lives – 'This, too, shall pass away.'

I have numbered my days. If God spares me to live to seventy, I have six thousand three hundred and eighty-eight left. I cannot live every one of them as though it is my last – that would drive me and my friends crazy but I can remember how short they are. And I can occasionally ask myself whether the things I am spending these days on are truly valuable, so that when I am old, I will look back on them with satisfaction.

In my office I have a day-planner. It is made up of small boxes, each has a date in it, and every day I am pulled from one box into another; today is 16 March and it dragged me from yesterday and into its territory. There is, however, a box for me that has no doors. I will not go from there to the next date. It is the day I will die. Now here is the big question of the universe, 'Does that box have no doors because it is a coffin and death is the end? Or does it have no doors because it has no walls and death is a beginning?'

Bertrand Russell, the atheistic philosopher, said, 'When I die I rot. There is darkness without and when I die there will be darkness within. Triviality for a moment, then nothing.' But from earliest times men and women have not believed that. When archaeologists discovered some of the oldest tombs on our planet they found the skeletons curled in a foetal position and encased in earthenware eggs; whoever had buried them was saying, 'One day you will live again.'

The story of Jesus is of somebody who had no fear of the final enemy. In fact he ruined every funeral he went to. He ruined Jairus's daughter's funeral, and the funeral of the young man who was restored to his widowed mother. He even ruined his own. Somebody had come into our world who had power over the last enemy. He could tell it when to go and cry out towards a tomb in the hillside – 'Lazarus come out!'[9] And he could tell it when to come – and so in his own death he 'gave up his spirit'.[10] He put it like this, '. . . I lay down my life – only to take it up again. No one takes it from me, but I lay it down of my own accord. I have authority to take it up again.'[11]

The book of Hebrews says a fascinating thing of him, 'By embracing death, taking it into himself, he destroyed the Devil's hold on death and freed all who cower through life, *scared to death of death*.'[12]

As I read the New Testament I sometimes get the feeling that Paul, who had met the risen Christ, is actually taunting the grim reaper:

> Death swallowed by triumphant Life!
> Who got the last word, oh, Death?
> Oh, Death, who's afraid of you now?[13]

Of course I'm apprehensive but I'm less afraid of death than I used to be. That, in itself, is strange, for my grown children, aching limbs and greying hair all whisper to me that the final enemy is getting nearer. But Christ is risen, the sting is drawn and death stands head down, robbed of victory. That belief has not stopped my grieving when I have lost somebody I love dearly; I miss them; sometimes I ache for them. But I do believe that death's triumph is not final and that the words John Donne wrote hundreds of years ago are prophetic indeed.

> Death be not proud though some have called thee
> Mighty and dreadful, for thou art not so,
> For, those, whom thou think'st thou dost overthrow
> Die not, poor death, nor yet canst thou kill me . . .
> One short sleep past, we wake eternally,
> And death shall be no more; *death thou shalt die.*

The idea that one day we shall 'wake eternally' was one I was taught in Sunday School but it was forty years later that an event occurred that moved the theology of

115

heaven from my head to my heart.

It was late on a Sunday evening that it happened. I had taken a group of teenagers on a beach barbeque but as they leapt from the cars to run to the sand one child lingered in the car. If only we had some warning of life-changing events perhaps we could get ready for them in some way, but that is not in their nature; such moments surprise us, sneak up on us, ambush us. It was so on this occasion.

Alicia, the girl who stayed, was fifteen and within six months would be dead. When she was fourteen she had contracted cancer. The chemotherapy had caused her hair to fall out, and when I sat with her that night it was just beginning to grow back; she looked stunning even with closely cropped hair. We could hear the sounds of shouts and screams in the distance as a typical youth group argued over who had found the largest piece of driftwood, but at that moment it was quiet in my car. I fumbled for something to say – 'Alicia, how are you coping with all this?'

And it was then that she said it. She had no idea what she was about to do; it did not enter her head that her words would be broadcast across the world, that radio and television would beam them to places she had never heard of. She did not know that men and women would catch their breath when they heard them, that people who had lost hope would be lifted.

I spoke them recently in Belfast in Northern Ireland. I stood on the stage of the brand-new Waterfront Centre, one of the finest concert halls in the world, in front of a packed audience. The spotlights were in my eyes and I couldn't make out the faces in the front row, let alone the thousands of others reaching right up into the gods. But I felt the faces, imagined the looks, sensed the emotion, caught a little of the hope as I shouted into the darkness beyond the lights the sentence that Alicia said to me that evening.

Alicia Owens said, '*I know where I'm going.*'

She was just fifteen and you may think her naive – but I don't. You may say, 'She had no idea of the pain ahead.' But she had already suffered much; she knew what lay ahead of her. No, the words of that child that night were not born out of shallowness, or immaturity. Alicia was looking the greatest enemy in the face and saying in her heart, 'You are not as fearsome as I first thought. You cannot hold me.'

As I drove home that night her words did not leave me. In fact, I think I knew even then that they never would. Alicia knew what kings and presidents do not know. She knew where she was going.

Was she deluded? I don't think so. She had decided that in this matter she was going to trust Christ. By any standards Jesus Christ is the most significant figure in the history of mankind. Einstein said of him, 'Here everything is extraordinary.' And what made him so extraordinary was that he had such a clear understanding of that other world. Philosophers have grasped for it, theologians have prayed to understand it; *he knew it.*

On the evening before he died he ate a meal with his disciples.[14] And it was at that meal he told them three things that brought their world crashing down around them. He said, 'One of you will betray me and one of

117

you will deny me.' Imagine what it must have been like for them; only twelve of them and yet there was a betrayer and a coward among them, but there was worse to come. He said, 'I am going to leave you, and where I am going you cannot come.' They had given up everything to follow him. They had left family, and businesses, they had been ridiculed and honoured. They had seen him heal the blind and raise the dead. He had sent them out to do his work but when they came back he was always there for them. And now he was going.

When my son was small and I was about to leave the house he would always shout, 'Can I come with you?' Peter, the disciple, does the same. He says to Jesus, 'Where are you going that I can't come?' And it was then, when they were at one of the lowest points of their lives, that he began to talk to them about another world. It was a world he understood; he knew where he was going. And he talked of it in terms of home. 'In my father's house are many rooms, if it were not so I would have told you. I am going to get it ready for you. I want you to be with me.'

It was as if he was saying, 'You must grasp that other world. You will not make sense of this one unless you do. This is not all there is.' You and I were meant to live with one eye on heaven.

Some months after our conversation in the car and as Alicia lay very near to death, I held her hand and told her I was going to dedicate a book to her that I had just written, called *The Sixty Minute Father*. I said, 'It will be to Alicia Owens – who knew where she was going.' She was pleased and smiled and I was honoured to do it, but neither of us had any idea that all over the world people would ask me to tell the story of that teenager's faith and her certainty in a world more real than this.

Shortly after her death I was asked to speak on the BBC and told listeners about Alicia and read something that seemed to capture the heart of her belief. It talks of death as our just passing over an horizon.

I am standing upon the seashore. A ship at my side spreads her white sails to the morning breeze and starts for the blue ocean. She is an object of beauty and strength, and I stand and watch her until at length she hangs like a speck of white cloud just where the sea and sky come down to mingle with each other. Then some one at my side says: 'There! She's gone.'

Gone where? Gone from my sight – that is all. She is just as large in mast and hull and spar as she was when she left my side, and just as able to bear her load of living freight to the place of destination. Her diminished size is in me, not in her; and just at the moment when someone at my side says, 'There! She's gone,' there are other eyes watching her coming, and other voices ready to take up the glad shout, 'Look! She comes!'[15]

Some years ago a missionary was returning to America after working in Africa for forty years. He had never had a furlough and as the boat pulled into New York harbour he wondered if there would be anybody to meet him. And then he heard some music. He thought, 'How lovely, they've got together a little band for me.' But then he realised that President Roosevelt was on the boat returning from a four-week safari in Africa, and it wasn't a little band, it was a big band.

Because of the President he was delayed and when he eventually stepped on to the dockside it was empty – there was nobody there to meet him. He went to a little hotel and fell by his bed weeping. He cried out, 'God, this President has been four weeks on holiday in Africa and he gets such a welcome back; I have served you forty years and for me there is no welcome home.'

And then he felt a voice whisper in his heart . . . 'You're not home yet.'

CHAPTER TEN

JUST OCCASIONALLY — I CAN HIDE

I may be wrong, but I have a hunch that when God wrote the Bible he made sure there were stories in it that children would never forget. These are accounts full of spiritual truth yet they get the attention of kids in a heartbeat. If you want to stretch your mind concerning the ultimate result of the battle between good and evil then grapple with the theology of Paul's letters, or plumb the depths of the book of Revelation. But if you are a Sunday School teacher and you want to show a class of nine-year-olds that when God and Satan fight there is no contest, take them to the first book of Kings and Mount Carmel. This is the 'high noon' of the Old Testament; four hundred and fifty prophets of Baal, and just one man of God — Elijah.

The two sides agree to put a sacrifice on an altar; the only thing missing is the fire. The one thing to be said in favour of both sides is that there was no compromise suggested; this was not an issue to be fudged. 'The God who answers by fire — he is God.'

I'm not sure if Sunday School teachers, rather like great conductors, have pieces that they specialise in, but nobody could tell the showdown on Mount Carmel like Mr Gardiner; he really wound the story up. I can hear him tell it now: 'The prophets of Baal cried to their gods for hours, and when there was no answer they began to dance around the altar. Perhaps they thought that would get their gods' attention' (we giggled). 'But still no fire. Then Elijah said, "Shout louder, perhaps your god is asleep" ' (we laughed).

And then Mr Gardiner's voice moved into horror story mode: 'When they still didn't get any response they began to cut themselves with swords and spears' (we grimaced), 'but it was all no use – no one answered, no one paid attention.'

Just as we were beginning to feel sorry for the prophets of Baal, Mr Gardiner produced Elijah. If it doesn't sound too irreverent, Mr Gardiner managed to make the prophet look like Clint Eastwood in robes.

' "This is too easy for my God", said Elijah. "Fill four large jars with water and soak the wood" ' (we gasped). ' "Now do it again" ' (we thought, don't push it, Elijah!). And then Mr Gardiner yelled so loud you almost thought he was Elijah, 'O Lord, God of Abraham, Isaac, and Israel, let it be known today that you are God in Israel and that I am your servant.' Mr Gardiner was silent, and we waited anxiously.

'Whooooosh – the fire falls!' (Simon Hargraves screamed because he thought his trousers were on fire.)

To me, as a small boy, Elijah was a hero and I will never forget the story of the battle on the mountain. But when I became a man I continued to read into the following chapter. If Mr Gardiner had told his story less well, it would have made it easier for me to cope with what I found there: 'Elijah was

*afraid. He sat down under a tree and prayed that he might die.
"I've had enough Lord, take my life." '*

*Could this be the same man my Sunday School teacher
brought to life for me all those years ago? Did men and women
who had fought and won great battles for God ever come to a
place where they felt like giving up – even on life itself? I doubt
that the child in Sunday School could have grasped it, but I
believe it now; it was the same man and sometimes we do come
to that place. And I thank God the Bible is so honest about its
heroes.*

—

I have often wondered what the psalmist was going
through when he cried out, 'Why are you downcast, O
my soul?'[1] Could it be that he was echoing an experience that others have attested to all through church
history? Some have called it 'the dark night of the soul'.
This is a time in our life when it seems that God, if he
is there at all, is far away. We may be plagued by doubts
about our faith, we find it hard to pray except to call out
to God for help, but so often it seems that heaven is preoccupied.

One of the most difficult things about such a time is
that while we are going through it, the world goes on. If
we are church leaders, there are sermons to preach (and
– even harder – to prepare), there are people to counsel,
and irony of ironies, doubters to encourage. If we are
involved in youth work, the fact that we are in a spiritual
desert doesn't stop the kids turning up on a Monday

night. If we are parents, our five-year-old still expects mum or dad to say prayers before bed. Life is going on; but we are dying inside.

In some ways we are glad life hasn't stopped and are grateful for the activity for, when we have gone through such times before, we have found the sheer act of getting on with life has helped us get through it. But now it doesn't seem to be working; we feel we are losing our grip on our faith. The incredible thing is that so often at the moment of greatest doubt and deepest spiritual depression, our faith is more important to us than anything else. We *want* to feel close to God. We *want* to believe.

Some years ago a book was published with an inspired title: it was called, *Honourably Wounded*.[2] The words referred to that category of soldiers in the last war who were discharged with full honour having suffered some injury in the service of their country. The author took up that theme and spoke of those who had suffered some hurt (often emotional breakdown) in Christian service. These faithful people had often served long and hard in trying to follow Christ but finally it seemed that their bodies had had enough, they could go on no longer; they were 'honourably wounded'.

Many Christians come into that category. I think of a young vicar and his wife. They had joined their new church with such enthusiasm and hope, firmly believing it was God's call on their lives. When I met with them they were broken, hurting and confused. It wasn't the battle against the forces of darkness that surprised them, rather the battleground that turned out to be *inside* the church they had come to lead. They were emotionally drained.

We are complicated beings and because of the very nature of the problem there are usually no easy answers. Such experiences are painful and at times excruciating in their intensity, but I doubt whether we can escape them completely. If we face them we can often find they produce a humility, and therefore a strength, that we might have lacked if the sun had never stopped shining. But it is not always necessary that they take us by surprise. When I have gone through those times I have observed, looking back, that they did not come quite out of the blue, but that in fact there were circumstances that, had I been a little more perceptive, may have given a hint as to what might be around the corner. Let me mention two.

CRITICISM

Oscar Wilde was once sent a letter by a theatre critic after the opening night of one of his plays. It read: 'You did not send me a ticket for your opening night. Perhaps you will be good enough to send one for your second night – if you have one.'

Wilde sent a note back: 'Please find enclosed two tickets for my new play. One is for you and the other for a friend – if you have one.'

But it's not just playwrights that have to face the critics. Each of us must live our lives in front of those who are waiting to give their verdict on our perform-ance. Our critics can be our greatest blessing and occasionally the opposite. The apostle Paul talks about this in his letter to the Christians who lived in Corinth.

> I care very little if I am judged by you or by any human court; indeed I do not even judge myself. My conscience is clear but that does not make me innocent. It is the Lord who judges me. Therefore judge nothing before the appointed time; wait till the Lord comes. He will bring to light what is hidden in darkness and will expose the motives of men's hearts. At that time each will receive his praise from God.[3]

Paul is talking about the three critics that every one of us will have to face. First there are others. They will tell you that you are too rich or too poor, too sombre or too jolly. They will tender their evaluation of your parenting, your prayer life and your waistline. Professor Lewis Smedes paraphrased Paul's attitude to his critics like this:

> You will evaluate my conduct and you will make an assessment of me, I know, and when you do I will listen to you. I know that you will size up my work; when you do, I will consider what you say. What you say and what you think about me matters to me. But I want you to know that after I have wrestled with my own conscience, after I have consulted my own convictions, and after I have made my decisions, your judgement will not matter much. It matters some, but not much. I will not rest my case with you.[4]

That is a vital principle. We would be wise to listen to our critics, but you can't live life looking over your shoulder wondering what they are making of your efforts – to live like that is to be imprisoned. One woman of seventy-five said, 'I have spent fifty years – half a century – imprisoned by other people's opinions of my life.'

Some years ago a woman said to me, 'Wouldn't it be ironic, with you and Dianne involved in a family ministry, if your own children went off the rails?' I may have imagined it but I thought I detected in her voice a slight hope that they would. The truth is, it wouldn't be ironic at all. Dianne and I have made many mistakes, but we have given the task of parenting our best shot and I won't live my life tormented by the opinions of others. Many church leaders face this. Their children are not allowed to be like other people's children. Because they are the leader's children the congregation demand they behave five levels above normal – and it's wrong.

I have generally found that one's critics fall into two categories. First, there are those who criticise in the hope of building you up. They may be misguided, but at heart they want your good. Listen to them, weigh what they say, and try their advice. These people will save you from tragedy, making a fool of yourself, and enable you to become even more effective. Even if it hurts, *it's worth it*: 'Wounds from a friend can be trusted.'[5]

Those in the second category criticise to bring you down. They do not have your long-term good at heart and they *enjoy* the criticism far too much. They will often preface biting remarks with lines like, 'I've got something I want to say to you in love', or 'You know how much I appreciate you, but lots of us are worried about . . .' They will rarely name the 'lots of us' and normally these are mythical characters that exist in the mind of the critic. You will find you can never please them, so don't try; they will wear you out. The last thing they want is for you to answer their difficulty because that would rob them of their ammunition. They are like the religious leaders of whom Jesus said, 'You are like children in the street playing games. You don't want to play weddings and you don't want to play funerals.'[6]

But according to Paul's list that leaves critic number two to deal with: ourselves. And it's here that Paul says a fascinating thing: 'I do not even judge myself. My conscience is clear but that does not make me innocent.' Of course the Bible tells us that it's good to examine our hearts, but not too much, and sometimes not too seriously, because we can fool ourselves.

In our home we have some bathroom scales. You can put weight on or take it off depending on how you stand on them. If you want to lose weight you lean to the left and push hard on the back of your foot. This simple action does away with the need to jog or eat salads. If you need to put on a few pounds you lean forward and press down. We will never get rid of them; all you need for the perfect figure is a little balance and the innate ability we all have to fool ourselves.

Somebody reading this book will wake up tomorrow morning, take a look in the mirror and exclaim, 'What a great face! What a privilege for the world to see that face today.' Almost everything they do during the day will be successful and when they fall into bed at the end of yet another triumphant twenty-four hours they will smile and say to themselves, 'You were awesome today.' Somebody else, also at present reading this book, will wake up tomorrow morning and they too will look in the mirror. They will sigh softly, look to heaven and say, 'Lord, you must have had so many noses to choose from, did I have to end up with this one? And were you so very short on eyebrows?' They will feel that they fail at everything they touch that day, and finally they will slump into bed feeling that somehow real life has passed them by.

The fascinating thing is, in terms of what actually occurred, both those days may have been exactly the same, but the individuals involved see them from the perspective of quite different personalities. We view our lives through certain coloured spectacles. Some of us are too hard on ourselves and some could do with a little more self-criticism. Try to understand the kind of person you are and try to make your evaluations more objective. Some of us are plagued by negative thoughts. Some typical ones are:

I must not show any weakness in this situation.
I must always act so that others will like me.
Most people are out to get me.
If I am really me, people won't like me.
I do not deserve to relax.

This is so often a battle of the mind. The Bible says, 'We take captive every thought to make it obedient to

Christ.'[7] That is, at the very least, a call to clear thinking which acknowledges a critic far higher than ourselves. And it is that third critic who is now waiting in the wings.

Paul says, 'It is the Lord who judges me.' One day the motives of every person's heart will be revealed and we will know for sure how we did. It is both sobering to realise that day will miss nothing, but it is also liberating to live in the knowledge of being judged by somebody who loves us completely.

The second issue that is so often at the heart of times of spiritual dryness is not very dramatic but that robs it of none of its potency to crush joy and peace from our lives.

SHEER FATIGUE

Many people today are exhausted. Often it is the accumulation of years in which we have tried to keep a myriad of activities going at once. We have been putting out chairs for the morning service, cutting sandwiches for the youth group and writing out new songs for the overhead projector at midnight on Saturday – and doing all of this while running a home, keeping down a job or perhaps dealing with the trauma of unemployment, and at the same time trying to tame a teenager. And we have just got tired.

Sometimes it's not until we try to relax that we realise how tired we are. I say 'try' because it's not that easy. Our body has got used to the thrill of adrenaline, and so we find it hard to sit still. We need to be active and, who would have believed it – we get ill on holiday. We wait all year for a summer break and for the first three days we are holed up in a bedroom on the Costa del Sol or, even more typically, we find that we *always* get 'flu at Christmas.

Most of us identify with this but there is another kind of tiredness, perhaps even a weariness, that can settle on us and make it hard to press on. Let me take you back for a moment to the psalmist and to something else he wrote at a time of incredible pressure. Before we read it let me remind you about this man. It was he who had taken on Goliath and won. Since that day he had fought battles for God that made the tussle against the giant seem trivial. He had battled against overwhelming odds both inside and outside the kingdom that had won his allegiance. He had faced treachery, betrayal and disappointment, but he was a man of courage and he had battled hard. David was a fighter.

But one day he wrote this: 'I will take refuge in the shadow of your wings until the disaster has passed.'[8] The image is the one Jesus used when he wept over Jerusalem: it is of a mother hen who suddenly senses danger. She spreads her wings wide and calls her little ones to run to her for safety. David says, 'God, do that for me. I have fought hard and long but I can't go on like this. Hide me in the shadow of your wings.' This is not a fighting image – you cannot win battles from this position – but it is a place of restoration, of peace, of safety; and it is for a season.

I have discovered in my life that there have been times when I could not go on as I had been. There have been occasions when I have heard Jesus say to me, 'Come apart and rest awhile.' My protests have sometimes been strong, 'But the crowds are still wanting us, and the gospel is still to be preached, and there are so many needs.' At such times I have sometimes felt his smile, not of reproof but rather of amusement, that I should have believed the responsibility for the whole kingdom sat squarely on my shoulders and that the God of whom it is written 'He said, "Let there be light" *and there was light*',[9] would find it hard to manage without me for a while.

At such times I have sat down with a cup of coffee and considered whether there are demands from which I can be released for a time. Sometimes this has involved going to colleagues and telling them openly how I am feeling and asking for their help. To do so I have had to battle with inner voices that whispered to me, 'But they're under pressure too,' and, most of all, with my pride.

Such times have meant that I have said 'No' to things in which I would loved to have been involved. I have sometimes cancelled things to create some space where I can breathe a little. On one occasion I was able to take a short break from the church leadership team that I was part of.

It was at such a time that a friend, observing a life of frenzied activity, said to me, 'You seem to have lost the ability to spend time with yourself.' He suggested that once a week I go for a walk in a nearby park and just 'kick the leaves'. He counselled me not to take a pen with which to jot down seminar ideas that might come to me, or even to feel the pressure to pray, but just to practise spending time with . . . me.

It seemed at first indulgent, and I would sometimes look around furtively to check whether the approaching jogger was somebody from our church who might be surprised that I had so much time on my hands. (It didn't occur to me that I might ask how come he had so much time on *his* hands!) But it wasn't just the guilt but rather that at first I found *I just couldn't do it.*

I had spent so much of my life 'doing' that just 'being' was proving harder than I thought. But we can learn, and 'kicking the leaves' became, for me, a phrase that summed up the art of creating space for ourselves – not just for our sakes, but so that we may be effective in the task to which God has called us. I believe the reason so many of us find it hard to spend time with God in silence or in prayer is that we have lost the ability to spend time with *ourselves*. We are busy people, we love activity, we cannot be still.

But a lifestyle of furious activity means the experience of what some call 'burn-out' may be not far from us. It is a picture of a match burned to the end of the wood, of a candle struggling bravely to keep a light alive but the wick is almost gone, or, in more modern terms, of a rocket engine that went off the launching pad with such force but fell away quickly, its energy expended. Somebody once said, 'Give me a busy life any day! I would rather burn out than rust out!' The truth is, you and I were meant to do neither. We were meant to 'last out' – to finish the course – not drop out exhausted after two laps. We were meant to complete the journey, be it long or short.

'I will take refuge in the shadow of your wings until the disaster has passed.'

Enjoy it. You may be there less time than you think.

CHAPTER ELEVEN

DON'T LOSE HEART

My last memory of Sunday School is not so much a lesson given by a teacher but a comment made by one . . . I was about to leave to begin my college course. I had said my 'goodbyes' to most of the teachers when down the aisle of the church came Mr Fisher who had taught me years ago. His back was stooped, but his handshake firm. He simply said, 'Keep the faith, Rob, and don't ever lose heart.'

It's quite a challenge. The world is filled with people who have lost heart. I have sometimes seen it in the eyes of somebody who has just lost their job. It's almost as if they have been robbed of dignity itself; sometimes they exhibit similar symptoms to grief at the loss of a loved one. I have seen it in the creeping despair of a parent who is consumed with worry over a teenager, and I have sometimes observed it in a church leader who can simply take no more.

To lose heart is often a precursor to losing life itself, for we lose the very will to live. And I have often seen those eyes of despair in the faces of the followers of Jesus. Somebody, some circumstance, or just the sheer accumulation of years of hardship have caused them to lose heart.

When I was a child I never saw a Sunday School teacher cry. I never knew a Sunday School teacher that ever had any doubts about his or her faith. I never had a teacher who said, 'I can't go on any longer – I'm through'. Now I am a man I wonder where my Sunday School teachers went to cry, and with whom they shared their doubts and how they dealt with the experience of your own heart crying out to you, 'It's time to give up.'

If this is how you feel then I want to help you to find heart again. If you were in my home I would sit you in my favourite chair, the one next to the fire, and I would endeavour with every fibre of my body to encourage you to keep pressing on. I wouldn't for a moment try to explain away, or dismiss, all you have been through that may have robbed you of joy, but I would want to lift your head and most of all I would want to tell you how precious you are to God.

I pray with all my heart that for somebody, today, perhaps even a Sunday School teacher somewhere, this last lesson will be rain in the desert.

I once lost heart in dramatic fashion. I noticed that our local leisure club was to hold a Tuesday 'keep fit' evening. I should have deduced from the title that it was designed for those who wanted to retain what they had already achieved, rather than for those for whom the concept was only a dream. That detail was lost on me and I went.

My son lent me a pair of trainers and I found a pair of tracksuit bottoms that I last used in form five at school. They seemed to have shrunk a little but nevertheless I donned the kit and set off.

The room was full. I have never seen such tiny waists and so much Lycra concentrated into such a small floor area. These creatures were rippling fitness. The instructor introduced herself and I stood listening whilst vainly trying to hold my stomach in and, at the same time, attempting to retrieve the cord of my joggers which had disappeared into the waistband.

She distributed tasks around the room and left me until last. It seemed she had decided I needed a little personal tuition. She told me she wanted to test my basic fitness before launching me on the terrors that most of the other Lycra wearers were now engaged in. She took my pulse and then asked me to leap up and down on what looked like a small orange box. I kept this up for all of a minute and then, seeing the colour in my face, and fearing the worst, she asked me to stop. She waited a short while and then took my pulse again.

Apparently if one is reasonably fit one's pulse returns to normal within two to three minutes. Mine came back on the following Thursday afternoon.

I had literally lost heart. If you had asked me to perform the simplest of functions when I had got off the orange box I couldn't have. With all the good will in the world *there was nothing left to give*.

Over the years I have observed, and at times, experienced some of the things that cause us to lose heart; I want to mention two in particular.

THE POWER OF THE PAST

The first is being dogged by the past. Dianne and I were engaged when I was twenty-one. I had just finished college and was penniless. And that wouldn't have been such a problem if I hadn't needed to buy an engagement ring. Now if I were counselling my own children in that situation I would advise that they get a job and save for the ring and, in so doing, they will make the experience more precious and more meaningful. It's good advice but it discounts the irrationality of love. I went to my bank manager.

Since that fateful day I have often had to deal with bank managers, but in those days I was a trifle naive in such matters. I'm not sure what I expected, but perhaps thought he might say, 'In love! How splendid! A penniless student – ideal! How much would you like?' Instead he smiled at me. It wasn't a warm, encouraging smile – rather the forced, wind-like smile of one who was about to say, 'If you don't get out of my bank fast, I'll call security.'

I borrowed the money elsewhere and we bought a second-hand ring. One year later we bought a wedding band in a discount jewellers, and we were married. Shortly after I qualified as a lawyer I bought Dianne an eternity ring. Those rings held such memories for us.

Just after our twenty-fifth wedding anniversary we were on holiday with our children and some friends.

The rest of us had been in the sea for some time when Dianne joined us. And it was then it happened. She threw a ball to me and suddenly something flashed in the sunlight. I watched as three rings, as if in slow motion, left Dianne's hand. They seemed to hover in the air for a moment and then disappeared into the sea. At the same time, she shouted, 'My rings!' and I saw a look of utter grief on her face. I know that in the great sweep of life there are things a lot bigger than losing a little jewellery, but it was more than that: it was the memories, the emotion that those things held – and they were gone.

Of course we searched, but the sea was rough and our efforts were futile. For days afterwards I walked along the edge of the water half expecting to see them lying there waiting to be reclaimed. We never did get those rings back. I often think of them lying somewhere, or perhaps by now on other hands, but still full of our memories. If they could talk they would tell how they have heard times of helpless laughter, and of crying that seemed to come from the very soul. In short, they hold the memories of two lives, each with successes and failures. If I am wise I will learn lessons from that past but in another sense I must let go of it and move on.

Our yesterdays have a strange power over us. One way they can cause us to lose heart is because we believe the future could never be as good as the past. As we look back it seems the summers were hotter, the trains more reliable, and life better in almost every way. In such a mood we can yearn for our church to be like it used to be, our teenagers to be toddlers again, and society to be as it was. Of course there may be sense in wanting those things, but the book of Ecclesiastes has in it a fascinating warning, 'Do not say "Why were the old days better than these?" For it is not wise to ask such questions.'[1] The past can trap us because it seems so good – we are tied to it. We refuse to face tomorrow because the memories of yesterday are so sweet.

Many a church leader is weary of people telling him or her how wonderful church used to be, many a child is tired of a parent reminding her how perfect her sister was when she was that age, and lots of people never move into new experiences because in their hearts they continually hanker after 'how it used to be'. The past may have been wonderful but usually it wasn't as great as our memory makes out, and in any event *it is still the past*. Mark Twain said, 'Plan for the future, it's where you're going to spend the rest of your life.'

But there is another problem of the past, and it is the opposite one. Some of us cannot face tomorrow because we are haunted by our yesterdays. With us it is not the problem of yearning for the years that have gone, but never being able to forget them. They remind us of sorrow and pain, perhaps failure and crushing disappointment. You may feel like that now. There is so much in life you would love to do but you crouch like a rabbit suddenly caught in the headlights of a car, unable to move forward or back. Because of the hurt or failure of the past you have lost the confidence to go on.

The story of the Bible is of God using ordinary men and women who achieved what they did in spite of, and not because of, what they were. Many of them had known pasts with shame and failure in them but they experienced the truth of a fascinating promise God gave Israel. That nation had known years of spiritual barrenness but he said to them, 'And I will restore to you the years that the locusts have eaten.'[2]

Imagine what it was like the day the locusts came. One moment the fields were full of wheat blowing in the wind and then you heard the sound. And after the sound came the darkness, as if the sun itself had given up in the face of the devastation that swept across the land. And when they were gone there was only ruin. The preparation, the sowing, the careful tending – all wasted. The hope of the harvest was dead.

Most of us go through a time in our lives when we identify with this. The years have taken their toll of us. We look back on disappointment, failure and heartache. We believe our life has been devastated. Such a situation may come about for many reasons. We may be victims of the wrongs of others, or our own wrongs may have caused us to pay a price we would never have imagined. It may be that illness or disappointments in our family have consumed our thoughts and drained us of effort. But God can change our lives: he can restore to us the years the locust has eaten.

This does not mean that suddenly life becomes easy, but it does mean that tomorrow does not have to be like yesterday. The times of darkness and nights of tears, the memories of past failure need not imprison us forever. This is true even if that devastation is because we have been foolish; even if the responsibility lies just with us. He is a God of new beginnings.

For the past three years I have presented a live seminar

based on the material in this book. The other day I received a letter from a woman who had been present at one of those events. She was a professional person, in her mid-fifties, and had only recently disclosed to a counsellor a rape that took place when she was twelve years old. This is part of what she wrote:

> I still struggle with the fact that I can be both loveable and loved, but slowly the truth dawns. Sometimes living has been like dying. Sometimes I have wanted to die. But I find at such times that God almost bombards me with the message that he loves me and values me. I now work for a Christian ministry and countless adults now approach me and tell of their own history of abuse and the new life they now seek. *My past has become a gift to help bring new life to others.*

And so God often does it. He takes a past that has in it only sorrow and uses it to bring joy. It is full of defeat but he uses it to lead others to victory. He redeems our yesterdays.

> I was regretting the past
> And fearing the future . . .
> Suddenly my Lord was speaking:
> 'MY NAME IS I AM.' He paused.
> I waited. He continued.
>
> 'WHEN YOU LIVE IN THE PAST
> WITH ITS MISTAKES AND REGRETS
> IT IS HARD. I AM NOT THERE.
> MY NAME IS NOT *I WAS*.

'WHEN YOU LIVE IN THE FUTURE
WITH ITS PROBLEMS AND FEARS
IT IS HARD. I AM NOT THERE.
MY NAME IS NOT *I WILL BE.*

'WHEN YOU LIVE IN THIS MOMENT
IT IS NOT HARD
I AM HERE.
MY NAME IS *I AM.*'[3]

When nothing makes sense

But even if we deal with our past there is another issue that time and time again forces us to lose heart. The clue to it is in something Paul wrote to the Christians who lived at Corinth:

> We are hard pressed on every side, but not crushed; perplexed but not in despair; persecuted but not abandoned; struck down but not destroyed.[4]

That's quite a list, but I think, of all those difficulties, the hardest to bear may have been '*perplexed*'. The literal meaning is 'at a loss as to know how to go on'. When you are hard pressed you know you are in a battle, when you are persecuted you can see the enemy, being struck down is a terrible thing, but at least you know where the blow came from. But 'perplexed'?

This is a time when we don't understand what is going on. It may even be a time when it appears God has left us, let us down, or in our lowest moments seems even to have betrayed us. It could be in the area of our prayer life. We had honestly believed God was going to answer our prayers with a resounding 'Yes!' The person we prayed for was so precious and we desperately wanted him to be well. And there were so many encouraging signs. We prayed the operation would be successful and it seemed to be; we prayed through every day of the treatment and, as time went by, we had a growing sense that all would be well. But our friend died. We accepted it, we even explained it to others, but in our own heart was a deep sense of perplexity and, if we were honest, a little anger.

Another root of perplexity may lie in disappointment as to what we have achieved in our ministry – in our work for God. It may be that as well as our job in the factory we have given time to teenagers. But the youth group that we used to lead is now scattered, and whereas at one time we believed these young men and women were going to grow into strong faith in Christ, it now appears they are disinterested. When we meet them in the street they seem embarrassed and mumble their reasons why they don't come to church any more. We look at a younger set of teens waiting to join our group and we wonder if we've got the stamina to do it all again when there seems such little fruit for our labours.

It may be you are a church leader. When you accepted the invitation to join your church you were sure that it was what God wanted. The people were welcoming, they promised to help with housing and babysitting, and constantly told you that God had answered their prayers in sending you. The honeymoon lasted six months: they never did get you the house they promised, they didn't manage babysitting beyond the first week, and it seems the only way God will answer their current prayers is for you to be called to another church. It has all gone so very wrong.

You honestly believed the change of job was God's will for your life. It was abroad, in fact in Africa, and you went willingly but after six months you became ill and had to return. You are devastated, embarrassed and perplexed.

You prayed so hard for your husband to find the faith that has so changed your life. Finally he agreed to come to church with you. To say it was an off-day would be an understatement. The preacher, who is normally compelling, seemed half-asleep, the drama was embarrassing and the welcome committee looked like piranhas in suits. When you got home he swore never to bother again.

There are no easy answers to such situations but part of the answer may lie in a sermon I heard when I was a teenager: the heart of it remains with me thirty years later. The preacher talked about, 'the non-fairy tale ending of the will of God'. He said that in life today happy endings are mandatory, but God sometimes looks at things from a different perspective. He takes a longer view, he is not in so much of a hurry as we are and, furthermore, he has a way of achieving things through brokenness that are harder crafted when we feel all is well. For that very reason we cannot say to the person who had to return from Africa after just six months, 'Ah, it obviously wasn't God's will for you to go there.' It may just have been God's perfect will.

Even more sobering is the fact that we cannot look at times of our life when things seems to be going well and presume we are therefore in the centre of God's will. If you are a business person be careful of saying, 'I must be doing what I should, look how my business is prospering.' His ways are higher than ours and his thoughts higher than our thoughts.

And we may be perplexed because of personal circumstances. Our family life may be very difficult, our children are a disappointment to us or we are in financial difficulty. It may be that we are a single person and our career is not going well – in fact we have been demoted, our friendships seem awkward and unfulfilling. Life is not good. It is easy at such times to lose heart and in so doing to lose our faith in God.

Those of us brought up in the Western world have been infected with a belief that makes all of this especially difficult. This belief is quite different to that taught to the majority of Christians through church history and yet in our culture it seems so fitting. It is simply that God exists to make us happy. When life goes well we feel close to him, when it goes badly we feel distant. And it is right here that one of the most fascinating of Jesus's parables may have something to say to us. 'Some (seed) fell on rocky places, where it did not have much soil. It sprang up quickly, because the soil was shallow. But when the sun came up, the plants were scorched, and they withered because they had no root.'[5] The sun speaks of persecution, of hard times, and the fascinating thing is the same sun that caused the good seed to grow caused the seed in shallow ground to die. Somebody says, 'Since I became a Christian, life has got worse, my family is going through a difficult time, my business is suffering, I can't go on in this faith. And somebody else in even worse circumstances says, 'Thank God that I know Him; if I didn't I could never get through it all.'

Not all our prayers will be answered with 'Yes'. Not all our children will turn out as we want, not all our churches will grow as we had hoped, and most of us will know times of crushing doubt. If you and I are to finish the course we are going to have somehow to learn how to hold on to God when our circumstances scream at us that there is no good reason to do so. This is not a new experience. Habakkuk wrote over three thousand years ago of this very period in our lives.

> Though the fig tree does not bud.
>   and there are no grapes on the vines,
> though the olive crop fails
>   and the fields produce no food,
> though there are no sheep in the pen
>   and no cattle in the stalls,
> yet will I rejoice in the Lord.[6]

This is not an easy-believism joy. This is not frivolous. This is not easy. This is faith that is tried while standing by a grave, or in unemployment, or when our children are breaking our hearts; it is faith that rises out of the ashes of our deepest disappointments. Sometimes at our lowest moments this faith sneaks up on us because we have nowhere else to go, and as surely as night follows day everyone of us will come to a place at some time in our lives where we go on believing, not just because God seems good to us, but in spite of the most crushing perplexity. At that moment alongside the giant of doubt comes the child of faith who ultimately looks up and cries, 'I don't understand but I still trust you.' At our lowest moments it may even allow us to cry out with Job, 'Though he slay me yet I will hope in him.'[7]

At the moment we 'see but a poor reflection as in a mirror'[8] but one day we will have perfect vision and understanding. And remember when we stand before him there will be some surprises. The work we did that seemed so fruitless may look a little different from that perspective, the disappointments of today may take on a different colour in five years' time, but perhaps even more so from the view of another world. And who knows what changes may be in store for the child who today breaks our heart; perhaps in parenting, as in life, we shouldn't read the score at half-time.

Well, my lessons are all declared. They are lessons of life and death and of that other world. They are experiences that have convinced me that in spite of who I am inside, God is not finished with me yet.

One woman put it like this:

'I know it all and I still love you.' That is the convincing, convicting, liberating truth that comes from an encounter with Christ. 'All is known. There is no need to pretend anymore.' I wrestled

with that truth, but it is hard to lay aside a mask
when it looks so like you and you have worn it so
long that you can't remember what you looked like
without it.[9]

Oh those masks, that hide the real us from others, and
even from ourselves. Like the circus clown we smile
while our hearts are breaking:

I have played the part so long,
Worn the make-up and the smile.
Took the bow and the applause,
Said, 'Oh fine, oh, yes, of course . . . I'm fine.'

Donned the costume, trod the boards,
Learnt the lines and sung the song,
Made you laugh and made you cry.
I have done it all so long . . .

I have done it all so long,
That I don't expect you see,
That to get this leading role,
The real cost was . . . me.[10]

You can take the mask off. God loves you. That is the
simple, irrational truth. It is true if you feel him so close
you could reach out and touch him. It is true if, at this
moment, you are in deep despair and he seems so very
distant. It is true if you have no love for him, or if you
have lost the love that was once so dear to you. You may
not believe in God – but God believes in you. He loves
you.

Our time together is almost over, but let me ask you to do something that I believe could be very significant. Following this chapter is an excerpt from Paul's letter to the church at Rome. Can I encourage you not to skip it, but to make yourself a cup of coffee, sit in your favourite armchair and, as you meditate on it, let its wisdom and challenge seep into your spirit? It seems to me so clearly to sum up the heart of the Christian faith. If this passage becomes our life goal we may not attain it all, but we will look back when we are old and be satisfied; and whatever our past, we can, by God's grace, begin to live these principles *today*.

There are many writings which have inspired me but the following two pieces are among my favourite prose in the whole world. The first comes from John White and is from the introduction to his book, *The Fight*. It sums up so much of what we have considered together:

As you live the Christian life, you may have periods of darkness or of doubt. You may encounter painful struggle and discouragement. But there will also be moments of exultation and glory. And most important of all, you will become free.[11]

And the second is from the words of Paul, the man who had such a keen sense of his own frailty, but who eventually fought a good fight, and who, by God's grace finished the course.

Therefore we do not lose heart. Though outwardly we are wasting away, yet inwardly we are being renewed day by day. For our light and momentary troubles are achieving for us an eternal glory that far outweighs them all. So we fix our eyes not on what is seen, but on what is unseen. For what is seen will only last a short while but what is unseen will last forever.[12]

Don't ever give up.

Lessons of life from the letter to the Romans

So here's what I want you to do, God helping you: Take your everyday, ordinary life – your sleeping, eating, going-to-work, and walking-around life – and place it before God as an offering. Embracing what God does for you is the best thing you can do for him. Don't become so well-adjusted to your culture that you fit into it without even thinking. Instead, fix your attention on God. You'll be changed from the inside out.

Readily recognise what he wants from you, and quickly respond to it. Unlike the culture around you, always dragging you down to its level of immaturity, God brings the best out of you, develops well-formed maturity in you.

I'm speaking to you out of deep gratitude for all that God has given me, and especially as I have responsibilities in relation to you. Living then, as every one of you does, in pure grace, it's important that you not misinterpret yourselves as people who are bringing this goodness to God. No, God brings it all to you. The only accurate way to understand ourselves is by what God is and by what he does for us, not by what we are and what we do for him.

In this way we are like the various parts of a human body. Each part gets its meaning from the body as a whole, not the other way around. The body we're talking about is Christ's chosen body of chosen people. Each of us finds our meaning and function as a part of his body. But as a chopped-off finger or cut-off toe we wouldn't amount to much, would we? So since we find ourselves fashioned into all these excellently formed and marvellously functioning parts in Christ's body, let's just go ahead and be what we were made to be, without enviously or proudly comparing ourselves with each other, or trying to be something we aren't.

If you preach, just preach God's Message, nothing else; if you help, just help, don't take over; if you teach, stick to your teaching; if you give encouraging guidance, be careful that you don't get bossy; if you're in charge, don't manipulate; if you are called to give aid to people in distress, keep your eyes open and be quick to respond; if you work with the disadvantaged, don't let yourself get irritated or depressed by them. Keep a smile on your face.

Love from the centre of who you are; don't fake it. Run for dear life from evil; hold on for dear life to good. Be good friends who love deeply; practise playing second fiddle.

Don't burn out; keep yourselves fuelled and aflame. Be alert servants of the Master, cheerfully expectant. Don't quit in hard times; pray all the harder. Help needy Christians; be inventive in hospitality.

Bless your enemies; no cursing under your breath. Laugh with your happy friends when they're happy; share tears when they're down. Get along with each other; don't be stuck up. Make friends with nobodies; don't be the great somebody. Don't hit back; discover beauty in everyone. If you've got it in you, get along with everybody. Don't insist on getting even; that's not for you to do. 'I'll do the judging,' says God. 'I'll take care of it.'

Our scriptures tell us that if we see our enemy hungry, we are to go and buy that person lunch, or if he's thirsty, get him a drink. Your generosity will surprise him with goodness. Don't let evil get the best of you; get the best of evil by doing good.[1]

Oh, the depth of the riches of the wisdom and knowledge of God!
How unsearchable his judgements, and his
  paths beyond tracing out!
'Who has known the mind of the Lord?
Or who has been his counsellor?'
'Who has ever given to God, that God should
  repay him?'
For from him and through him and to him are
  all things.
To him be the glory forever! Amen.[2]

NOTES

Every effort has been made to locate sources and to seek permission for the use of quotes. In cases where this has not been possible, we apologise and will do all we can to rectify the situation in subsequent editions.

CHAPTER ONE: THE KISS OF GOD

1. See Psalm 103:12.
2. Luke 7:36–50.
3. John Bunyan, *Pilgrim's Progress.*
4. Luke 15:11–32.
5. Luke 11:4 (paraphrased).
6. See Matthew 18:23–35.
7. Luke 23:34.
8. Luke 23:42.
9. Luke 23:43.

10. Gwilym Hiraethog (translated by Robert Lowry), 'Here is love'.

CHAPTER TWO: I AM KNOWN COMPLETELY AND LOVED UNCONDITIONALLY

1. Personal correspondence.
2. Allan Ahlberg, 'Picking Teams', *Please Mrs Butler – Verses by Allan Ahlberg* (Puffin, 1983). Reproduced by permission of Frederick Warne & Co.
3. See Romans 8:38-9.
4. Jeff Lucas, *Walking Backwards* (Scripture Union, 1997). Used by permission.

CHAPTER THREE: THE GREATEST FREEDOM IS IN HAVING NOTHING TO PROVE

1. Materials from *When I Relax I Feel Guilty* (Chariot Victor Publishing, 1979). Used by permission.
2. Personal correspondence.
3. From an article in *Leadership* journal.
4. Henry Nouwen, *The Genesee Diary* (Doubleday, 1989).

CHAPTER FOUR: TOMORROW BELONGS TO THE FAILURES

1. Annie Johnson Flint, 'He Giveth More Grace'.
2. John 15:5 (New King James version).
3. Luke 22:60-2.
4. Luke 22:31-2.
5. Acts 4:20.
6. Psalm 50:10-12.
7. Luke 2:41-50.

8. Luke 2:44-5 (Authorised Version).

CHAPTER FIVE: WHEN YOU PLAY TO YOUR STRENGTHS THE GIANTS FALL FASTER

1. 1 Samuel 17:26ff.
2. John 6:15 (paraphrased).
3. Luke 12:13–14 (paraphrased).
4. Mark 1:37–8 (paraphrased).
5. 1 Corinthians 12:17.
6. Donald Clifton and Paula Nelson, *Play to your Strengths: Focus on what you do best and success will follow* (Piatkus, 1994).

CHAPTER SIX: DON'T SPEND YOUR LIFE WISHING YOU COULD HAVE DONE MORE

1. 1 Corinthians 1:27–9.
2. Based on John 6:1–13.

CHAPTER SEVEN: I WAS MEANT TO PARTY WITH MY ENEMIES

1. John 13:1ff.
2. John 13:14.
3. John 13:34.
4. 1 Corinthians 1 from Eugene Peterson, *The Message* (Navpress, 1993).
5. John 17:11.
6. James 4:11 (*The Message*).
7. With thanks to Dave Phillips, Focus on the Family, Canada. Author unknown.

8. By Milton Olsen. Publication unknown.
9. John 17:1–21.

CHAPTER EIGHT: SOMETIMES ANSWERS AREN'T THE LAST WORD

1. Matthew 27:30.
2. Matthew 27:46.
3. Job 38:1–40:5 (paraphrased).

CHAPTER NINE: YOU'RE NOT HOME YET

1. C.S. Lewis, *The Last Battle* (Harper Collins).
2. Ecclesiastes 3:8.
3. Ecclesiastes 3:2.
4. Psalm 90:10.
5. Psalm 90:12.
6. Ecclesiastes 2:18–19.
7. James Dobson, News from Focus on the Family.
8. J. Shirley, 'Death the Leveller', *The Golden Treasury* (Oxford University Press, 1964).
9. John 11:43.
10. John 19:30.
11. John 10:17–18 (paraphrased).
12. Hebrews 2:14–15 (*The Message*).
13. 1 Corinthians 15:55 (*The Message*).
14. John 13:8–14:4.
15. Author unknown.

CHAPTER TEN: JUST OCCASIONALLY – I CAN HIDE

1. Psalm 42:5.
2. Marjory Foyle, *Honourably Wounded* (Monarch).
3. 1 Corinthians 4:3-5.
4. Lewis Smedes, *How Can It be All Right When Everything Is Wrong?* (Lion, 1982).
5. Proverbs 27:6.
6. Luke 7:32 (paraphrased).
7. 2 Corinthians 10:5.
8. Psalm 57:1.
9. Genesis 1:3.

CHAPTER ELEVEN: DON'T LOSE HEART

1. Ecclesiastes 7:10 (Authorised Version).
2. Joel 2:25 (Authorised Version).
3. Helen Mallicoat, 'I Am', in Tim Hansel, *Holy Sweat* (Word, 1987), p. 136.
4. 2 Corinthians 4:8–9.
5. Matthew 13:5.
6. Habakkuk 3:17–18.
7. Job 13:15.
8. 1 Corinthians 13:12.
9. Sheila Walsh, *Honestly* (Hodder & Stoughton, 1996). Used by permission.
10. Poem by Rob Parsons.
11. John White, *The Fight* (Inter-Varsity Press, 1977).
12. 2 Corinthians 4:16–18.

LESSONS OF LIFE FROM THE LETTER TO THE ROMANS

1. Romans 12 (*The Message*).
2. Romans 11:33–6.

Also by Rob Parsons:

The Money Secret

'Not just a book on debt — but on life choices.
This is unmissable.'
ANTONY ELLIOTT

The secret is as old as time itself, and no amount
of money can replace its power. The poor who
find it know financial security, the wealthy who
despise it end life as paupers.

You will treasure this wisdom long after you have
finished the last page. If you are in debt it will help
you get out, if you are financially secure it will
help you be wise with your money, and if you feel
that nobody could understand the sheer loneliness
of financial pressure, then *The Money Secret* will
become your friend.

Hodder & Stoughton
ISBN 0 340 86277 7

The Sixty Minute Father

An Hour to Change Your Child's Life

'*A book that helps you achieve
the most important success of all.*'
SIR JOHN HARVEY-JONES

The Sixty Minute Father sets goals that can help every
father ensure that he doesn't miss out on the
greatest opportunity of his life.

- Put dates in your diary that are important for your
  children
- Talk to your baby as if she understands every word
- If you have to be away, write your child a letter
- Kneel to talk to toddlers and listen with your eyes
- Tell them how you spend your day

Full of practical advice, *The Sixty Minute Father* can be
read in about an hour but could change your
child's life forever.

Hodder & Stoughton
ISBN 0 340 63040 X

The Sixty Minute Marriage

Transform Your Relationship in One Hour

'*Wise and witty. Full of down-to-earth advice that works.*'
LYNDA LEE POTTER

'*Sixty minutes of laughter, tears and honesty.
This life-changing book should be compulsory
reading for every couple.*'
STEVE CHALKE

Following the huge success of *The Sixty Minute Father*,
Rob Parsons presents an action plan to
revolutionise every relationship.

* Are affairs good for a marriage?
* How to deal with a partner who just won't talk things through
* How to argue – effectively
* Why many men say, 'My wife's not interested in sex'
* Why cutting your credit card in half could save your marriage
* How a divorce will affect your children

Hodder & Stoughton
ISBN 0 340 67145 9

The Sixty Minute Mother
talks to Rob Parsons

'Every mother should read this book – it's fantastic!'
DIANE LOUISE JORDAN

Rob Parsons, in the company of mothers from all walks of life, takes us on a fascinating journey into the world of motherhood alongside working mums, stay-at-home mums, single parent mums and 'I can't believe that my test kit turned blue' mums. We meet 'ordinary mum' on her way to work with stewed prune in her hair and her dress caught in the back of her tights; coming in the other direction is 'super mum', who returns library books a week early, knows the school holiday dates and loves making models out of toilet rolls.

Issues addressed in this book include:

- I think I'm a good mum so why do I sometimes feel so guilty?
- Is it unusual to be singing Postman Pat at the office?
- Should I work full time or stay at home?
- My kids are now teenagers – what happened?
- I love my kids but is it all right not to like them occasionally?

Hodder & Stoughton
ISBN 0 340 63061 2

Also by Rob Parsons:

The Heart of Success

Making it in business without losing in life

'This book redefines the concept of success. It has some answers for people who are succeeding in business but beginning to ask themselves whether there is more to life than they are currently achieving. It could change your life if you dare act on the thoughts it raises for you. I would recommend CEO's to give a copy of this book to every manager in their company.'

JIM WRIGHT, VICE-PRESIDENT OF HUMAN RESOURCES, SMITHKLINE BEECHAM R&D

'Rob Parsons is one of the most inspirational speakers in the country today. *The Heart of Success* has the same ingredients as his presentations – motivating, practical and giving you a sense that somebody has just turned a light on.'

ROSEMARY CONLEY, AUTHOR, BROADCASTER AND CHAIRMAN OF THE ROSEMARY CONLEY GROUP

'*The Heart of Success* is hard to put down and impossible to ignore. It has the ability not just to improve the performance of your company but your life as well.'

CHRIS STREET, VICE-PRESIDENT AND GENERAL MANAGER OF GLOBAL CUSTOMER SERVICES, ALCATEL

For further information visit:
<u>www.letsdolife.com</u>

Hodder and Stoughton
ISBN 0 340 78623 X